AGE-PROOF
YOUR MIND

AGE-PROOF YOUR MIND

Detect, Delay, and Prevent Memory Loss—Before It's Too Late

ZALDY S. TAN, MD, MPH

WARNER BOOKS

NEW YORK   BOSTON

The stories and people depicted in this book are fictional composites of many individuals that the author has met over the years. They do not represent any one person or group of people. Similarities to any one person or persons are purely coincidental and unintentional.

Neither this nor any other program should be followed without first consulting a health care professional. If you have any special conditions requiring attention, you should consult with your health care professional regularly regarding possible modification of the program contained in this book.

Warner Books

Time Warner Book Group
1271 Avenue of the Americas, New York, NY 10020

Printed in the United States of America

ISBN 0-7394-5738-1

Book design by Giorgetta Bell McRee

To Rudy and Julita

Contents

Acknowledgments

An endeavor such as this would not have been possible if not for the support of countless people who have helped me along the way. I especially want to acknowledge the contributions of Dr. George Rebok of the Johns Hopkins University, who put his many years of research experience to work in helping develop the innovative memory improvement and workout programs presented in this book. I thank my agent, Stedman Mays of Scribblers House LLC, for his encouragement and advice. His colleague Mary Tahan was also helpful in the early stages of this project. Thanks also to Dr. Bradley Willcox of the Okinawa Centenarian Study for pointing me to the right direction. My editor at Warner Books, Diana Baroni, gave me positive feedback that helped shape this project into a better book. Sayaka Mitsuhashi contributed her knowledge of nutrition and her skills in recipe writing to this book. I extend my gratitude to Susanne Klingenstein of the Harvard-MIT Division of Health Sciences and Technology, to my classmates at HST 960, and to my mentors and colleagues at the HMS Division on Aging, the Beth Israel Deaconess Medical Center, the Hebrew Rehabilitation Center, and the Framingham Heart Study for their insightful comments and suggestions. I thank my students, whose intellectual curiosity and idealism serve as a constant source of inspiration to educators like me.

I thank my family, Rudy & Julita, Jerry & Jackie, Kenneth & Debbie, Addison & Susan, Teddy & Veronica, my nieces and nephews for their love, patience, and understanding. Finally, I acknowledge the assistance and inspiration from all my patients, past, present, and future, and their families—who are the real unsung heroes to whom I tip my hat.

Introduction

Dr. Alan Zarkin squinted, closely inspecting the result of his handiwork. Under the bright operating room light, his patient's iodine-coated skin glistened. The sutures that approximated the "bikini" skin incision he had made to deliver Liana's healthy baby were perfectly symmetric: Each one was equally as far from the one that preceded it as from the one that followed it; the ends were cut exactly half a centimeter from the skin surface.

"I did such a beautiful job, I'll initial it," proclaimed Dr. Zarkin.

In one swift move, he picked up the scalpel from the tray and proceeded to carve a three-inch-tall letter A followed by a Z on Liana's skin, as any artist would his masterpiece. The surgical team who witnessed the inexplicable mutilation in the operating room gave a collective gasp. And when the news broke out on the front page of major newspapers, that gasp was repeated by the rest of the world. Unbeknownst to his patient, the veteran obstetrician had already been the subject of several complaints about erratic behavior. In fact, Dr. Zarkin had been suspended five months earlier by the prestigious Manhattan hospital where he practiced. The doctor's list of bizarre behaviors allegedly included screaming at coworkers and "pulling and yanking a newborn infant's arm and legs after delivery." In the legal onslaught that followed the infamous incident, Dr. Zarkin's lawyer revealed that his client had been suffering from a serious degenerative brain condition similar to Alzheimer's disease. Nobody knows for sure whether the doctor had had ominous signs of a memory problem before he exhibited this bizarre behavior and whether he and the people around him simply chose to ignore it. However, because the typical course of a degenerative brain disease is best characterized as slow and smoldering over many years, red flags of a failing mind probably existed long before this regrettable event. Whenever I recall this case, I can't help but wonder: How many Dr. Zarkins are living among us?

Most people are blissfully unaware of their own chances of getting Alzheimer's disease, much less if they already have the earliest stages of it. While they know their last cholesterol level and blood pressure, they are oblivious to the status of their memory and cognitive abilities. The thought of having progressive memory loss provokes feelings of fear and denial in many of us. Thus, early warning signs are often too easily dismissed by rationalization and swept under the rug of borrowed time. In the back of the minds of millions of aging Americans is a lingering question. When they misplace their keys or find that they have to circle the lot for fifteen minutes to locate their parked car, they secretly worry. When the health reporter on the nightly news announces cutting-edge research that claims to be able to detect early Alzheimer's disease, they turn up the volume. And as they watch the quick-witted man or woman of their childhood fade away before their eyes, they wonder if they and their children are destined to suffer the same fate, and how long they have before it gets them.

Each year in the United States, an estimated 360,000 new cases of Alzheimer's are diagnosed. With the average life expectancy increasing, the number of Americans with Alzheimer's disease is expected to triple in the next forty years.[1] And as many of us look forward to living to a hundred, we must also face the fact that one out of two people over the age of eighty-five has Alzheimer's. Scientists used to call occasional lapses of memory *benign forgetfulness*, which they considered to be part and parcel of normal aging. Now it is known that subtle memory lapses may be heralding the appearance of Alzheimer's disease a few years down the road. A specific set of criteria defines this very early dementia, known in scientific circles as mild cognitive impairment or MCI. Without treatment, up to half of people with MCI will progress to Alzheimer's disease in just three to four years. More than ever, it is important to identify individuals who have MCI—they are the ones most likely to benefit from interventions that can delay or even prevent the progression of irreversible memory loss.

In this book, I will present the latest scientific research on the prevention, early detection, and treatment of memory loss. The first part of the book will explore the beneficial and adverse factors that influence the development of the human mind by promoting its preservation or threatening to undermine its future. These include novel scientific concepts such as brain plasticity and mild cognitive impairment (MCI), two of the most promising areas of memory and brain aging research. In part 2, I will interpret and summarize the latest breakthrough discoveries on the role of diet, physical and mental exercise, estrogen replacement therapy, and antioxidant and anti-inflammatory medications in delaying or preventing age-related memory decline and Alzheimer's disease.

1. Ernst RL, Hay JW. The US economic and social costs of Alzheimer's disease revisited. *Am J Pub Health* 1994;84:1261–1264.

In part 3, I will help you identify your own risk for Alzheimer's disease and provide you with a way to assess the present status of your mind. The Memory Stress Test, a comprehensive set of tests designed to help you identify your mind's unique set of strengths and weaknesses, also has the potential of identifying early signs of memory loss when taken regularly. I will also propose a ten-step multimodal approach to age-proofing your mind that includes powerful memory improvement techniques and a Sixty-Minute Brain Workout especially developed for this book to sharpen your mental abilities.

At this early juncture, I should emphasize that most of the information I will be presenting in this book represents cutting-edge research and is not meant to substitute for medical evaluation by a trained professional. Only a physician who has personal knowledge of your situation can tell which interventions are right for you.

Learning anything new requires the formation of new connections between brain cells. Thus, if you remember anything at all from this book six months from now, it will be because your brain was physically changed by the new information. I invite you to forget what you think you know about remembering and forgetting, and to allow me to physically alter the circuitry of your brain through the information I have written in these pages.

"Men ought to know that from the human brain, and the brain only, arises our pleasures, joys, laughter, and jests as well as our sorrows, pains, griefs, and tears. It is the same thing, which makes us mad or delirious, inspires us with dread and fear, whether by night or by day, brings us sleeplessness, inopportune mistakes, aimless anxieties, absent-mindedness and acts that are contrary to habit. . . ."

—HIPPOCRATES, "ON THE SACRED DISEASE," 400 B.C.[1]

1. Translated by Francis Adams. http://classics.mit.edu/Hippocrates/sacred.html.

PART I

Are You Losing Your Mind?

At some point, we have all questioned whether the occasional episodes of forgetfulness we experience in the course of our daily lives are simply signs of normal aging or are heralding the appearance of something more ominous, such as Alzheimer's disease. When should we start worrying about our memory abilities, and what can we do about them?

In the following chapters, I will help you get better acquainted with the different patterns of mental aging, including the role of brain plasticity and mental wear and tear in explaining why some people remain intellectually sharp well into their old age while others around them succumb to Alzheimer's disease. I will provide you with answers to some of your most basic questions, such as how memories are made and how they are forgotten. In the last chapter of this part of the book, I will introduce you to a condition known as mild cognitive impairment (MCI), the earliest warning sign of the impending appearance of Alzheimer's disease in the next few years, and how you can identify if you or a loved one is on the edge of this slippery slope of memory decline. If you've ever had concerns about your memory, it is time to stop worrying and start reading the following chapters to know what changes you can expect with your mind in the next few years.

PART I

Chapter 1

Wrinkles of the Mind

*"If the brain were so simple we could understand it,
we would be so simple we couldn't."*

—LYALL WATSON

Welcome to the club. If you picked up this book, you probably are one of the millions of people around the world who is beginning to worry about his memory. Lapses in memory that become more frequent with the passage of time lead many of us to question why our memory isn't as sharp as it used to be. How many names are we allowed to forget? How many times can we misplace our keys and glasses? And how many minutes should it take us to locate a parked car before we need to start worrying about the state of our minds?

When I was a twenty-two-year-old freshman in medical school, I spent many days sitting through series of hour-long lectures given by a succession of wise elderly doctors, their monotonous voices reverberating through the walls of the lecture hall. Although I never thought anything of it at that time, I now look back with fascination on my ability to accumulate a sizable wealth of technical knowledge within a relatively short span of time. Like a sponge, my brain absorbed enormous amounts of esoteric medical information. At the time, I suspected that I might never find any practical use for much of this information in my medical practice. But my brain held on to the data just the same. The fact that I can still remember things I learned many years ago is a testament to the remarkable efficiency of young brains to acquire, process, retain, and ultimately retrieve new information.

As we get older, it is not unusual to sense a subtle but perceptible dip in our ability to acquire and retain new information. For instance, it may take us a few seconds longer to process and retrieve certain types of information, such as our ATM number or the date of our next dental checkup. In an age when overlapping appointments and back-to-back meetings are the norm, many of us have become willing hostages to various forms of memory crutches. If you don't believe me, just think of how you felt the last time you misplaced your date book or how disorganized your day was when your secretary called in sick. The popularity of Post-it notes, car dashboard computers that make irritating noises when you leave the key in the ignition, and the ubiquitous FORGOT YOUR PASSWORD? button on Web sites all help to keep our imperfect memories from interfering with the flow of our busy lives. With our generation's increasing dependency on memory crutches now, have you ever wondered about the fate of your memory in the next ten or twenty years?

Many consider a sharp memory to be just one of the vestiges of youth that we should expect to part with sooner or later. This feels even truer for those who have been silent witnesses to the blunting of the memory of a forgetful parent or grandparent. But if memory problems and aging are truly inseparable and everyone is destined to become forgetful eventually, how can we explain the not-so-uncommon observation that many older people such as Georgia O'Keeffe, Winston Churchill, Golda Meir, George Burns, and Strom Thurmond somehow managed to remain mentally sharp well into their ninth and tenth decades?

DESTINED TO FORGET?

While we have learned to accept the reality that excellent physical health is fleeting, we all hope to at least be able to hold on to our memory and to take it with us when the time comes for us to make our exit. For many, a healthy mind trumps a healthy body anytime.

In reality, many of the diseases that we commonly consider as part of aging, whether these be arthritis, impotence, or Alzheimer's, are *not* inevitable. For a disease to be truly unavoidable, it should be expected and observed to appear in everyone who reaches or goes beyond a certain age. Yet we know that among us are people who will be able to bake the cake to celebrate their hundredth birthday, while others will succumb to Alzheimer's disease and not even remember their sixty-fifth.

Some scientists believe that in the absence of disease, we should all be able to maintain our mental abilities well into old age. Others think that memory decline is part and parcel of normal aging and that the rate of decline is the only thing that distinguishes the mind of the diseased from that of the normally aging. The truth is probably somewhere in between. While it is theoretically possible (with the combination of perfect genes, ideal environmental conditions, and a healthy dose of luck) to completely dodge the memory changes that typically accompany aging, most of us are likely to develop age-related changes in memory performance to a certain degree. These changes can be observed and measured by standard memory and psychological tests. However, this does *not* mean that everyone is destined to have *noticeable* changes in their memory during the course of their everyday lives. In this book, you will find tests designed to help you detect early signs of memory problems. I will also outline how relatively simple changes in your diet can help in warding off premature memory loss. The Sixty-Minute Brain Workout will provide you with mental exercises that can strengthen specific areas of brain weakness. The important thing to remember is that there are things you *can* do to tip the odds of memory preservation versus decline decidedly in your favor. You are *not* destined to become forgetful.

Arguably, no other part of our body is as unique or complex as our brains. Its strengths, weaknesses, thoughts, and experiences are so distinct that making absolute statements on what is normal and what is not is next to impossible. One of the biggest challenges in identifying people with abnormal memory loss is determining where to draw the line that will effectively distinguish the normal changes in memory that occur with aging from those that characterize very early Alzheimer's disease. To appreciate the remarkable complexity and uniqueness of our brains, let's take a step back and get better acquainted with the origins of this mysterious organ.

THE SIXTY-FIVE-MILLION-YEAR-OLD BRAIN

If I ask you to tell me your last cholesterol and blood pressure levels, you probably won't have too much difficulty in coming up with the numbers. Many people routinely mark down the dates for their next mammogram, colonoscopy, Pap smear, or PSA with red ink in their calendars to emphasize the importance of these health screening procedures to the maintenance of their health. Yet if I ask you to tell me the status of your memory, you would probably scratch your head and tell me that you have no idea.

Have you ever wondered why, despite all the high-tech medical advances in our generation, we still cannot take a test that will tell us the state of our minds, much the way simple tests can tell us the state of other vital organs such as our hearts? From looking at a set of squiggly lines on a strip of paper, a cardiologist can immediately tell how well your heart is functioning. The electrocardiogram (EKG) is a quick, simple, and inexpensive piece of equipment found in many doctor's offices that can detect an enlargement of the heart, spot irregularities in its rhythm, and even catch an evolving heart attack. Unfortunately, there is currently no equivalent test that can tell us how well the brain is functioning. Thus, the best way to get to know how well your mind is functioning is to periodically monitor the accuracy and efficiency by which you can tackle challenging intellectual tasks, such as those presented in the Memory Stress Test. But before you do that, you must first gain a better understanding of how your brain normally functions. Only by acquiring this basic knowledge will you understand what the different tests tell you about your mind. Recognizing how the brain normally functions will then allow you to recognize the first signs of problems when they appear.

For starters, the brain is a three-pound walnut-shaped mass inconspicuously hidden behind the bony skull. Compared with the heart, the brain is an infinitely more complex organ. Unlike the dynamic heart, which sits in the center of the body, ready to physically respond to the calls of joy and sadness, love and anger, valor and fear, the brain does its job quietly and efficiently, without much drama or fanfare. Thus, it is not too difficult to see why early civilizations quickly dismissed it as a nonessential organ that served no real purpose other than perhaps to fill space or cool the blood.

Of course, we now know that the brain is much more than the body's equivalent of a car radiator. It is a sophisticated and powerful organ that is the product of millions of years of evolution, exerting control and dominance over the rest of the body. The origin of the modern human brain can be traced back to more than sixty-five million years in the past, roughly to the time when dinosaurs became extinct and mammals became free to roam the earth.

Compared with other mammals, members of the primate family, which includes monkeys, apes, and of course humans, have larger, heavier, and more complicated brains. The human species is believed to have evolved from land-dwelling chimpanzees over a period of only about one hundred thousand years. Considering the amount of intellectual evolution that must occur to allow us to surpass the abilities of our most intelligent cousins in the primate family, it took a relatively short span of time for the modern human brain to emerge. In fact, we still share 98 percent of our genetic codes with chimpanzees, and certain structures of the human brain have changed very little or not at all from its primate origin.

THE MASTER OF THE MIND

From its primitive past, one part of the brain has evolved so completely and effectively that it is credited with shooting the human species straight to the top of the evolutionary tree. The *cerebral cortex* is the most highly differentiated of all the areas of the human brain. The cortex, which literally translated means "rind" or "peel," is the outermost layer of the brain. It is a relatively small structure, with an area of only approximately two thousand square centimeters (roughly equivalent to that of a car's hubcap). But cramped in this small area are more than fifteen billion brain cells or *neurons* and an even greater number of supporting or *glial* cells, which nourish and protect the brain cells from damage. To communicate with each other, each neuron makes more than a thousand connections called *synapses* to others like it, forming an interweaving network that transmits vital information throughout the intellectual superhighway.

The cerebral cortex is the true center of human intelligence. It is also the prime target of degenerative diseases such as Alzheimer's, which threaten to knock us down several notches from our comfortable perch high up on the evolutionary tree. Its peculiar vulnerability to disease can be explained by the exquisite sensitivity to damage of the brain cells that live there. As we age, an increasing number of these brain cells succumb to cumulative damage, with a resulting decrease in brain reserves. These changes make older people more susceptible to memory loss and decline in other mental abilities. Thus, prevention efforts against memory problems seek to protect the delicate brain cells of the cerebral cortex from harmful agents and degenerative diseases.

I should emphasize that the aging process itself *will not* cause you to develop Alzheimer's disease. Brain aging is not a disease; rather, it is just a part of human development that begins at the moment of conception and ends at the time of death. Studies have shown that the ever-changing human brain continues to transform itself even in the late stages of life. However, at no time in the human life cycle is the brain more dynamic than during the first few years of life. In fact, the pattern of early brain development provides us with some valuable insights that will help us to better understand the mysteries of the aging brain.

THE AGING BODY AND BRAIN

When most people think of aging, stereotypical images such as gray hair, wrinkled skin, and a stooped posture readily come to mind. But beneath the skin's surface, our internal organs also experience dramatic changes with age. During infancy and childhood, our various organ systems grow and mature. With the notable exception of the brain, they reach their functional peak during late adolescence and early adulthood. They then enter a plateau period that typically extends from early adulthood to middle age. It is during this reproductive period of life that organ systems are functioning at their optimal level.

By the time we reach middle age, our bodies have begun to show signs of wear and tear—and we feel it. The heart, kidneys, lungs, liver, and virtually all other organs go through such age-related changes. The kidneys, for instance, lose 20 to 30 percent of their weight between the ages of thirty and ninety years, and their length shortens by half a centimeter for each decade after age fifty. Though continuing to function normally, many of our internal organs become more vulnerable to disease. Physically active older people, such as former professional athletes, notice that even though they continue to exercise, their muscles still become smaller and less prominent compared with when they were younger. This is explained by the normal decrease in muscle mass with age that is largely independent of the level of a person's physical activity. For the same intensity and frequency of exercise, the muscles of a sixty- or seventy-year-old simply cannot get as large and as strong as those of people in their early twenties.

The Shrinking Brain

The maximum weight of the brain is attained at around age twenty and remains relatively stable until about age forty. But under the microscope, scientists have seen brain cells start to die as early as age thirty. Estimates show that by late middle age, we are losing an average of about 1 percent of our brain cells every year. In fact, between the ages of eighteen and ninety-five, the human brain is estimated to lose 57 percent of its brain cells. Because our skulls typically do not shrink with age, the lost brain tissue is replaced by fluid and dead space, leaving large, dark holes where healthy brain tissue used to be.

Parallel to the loss of muscle mass and strength, there is also a corresponding connection between brain volume and age. The brain of a young person looks like a complicated mass of wrinkled fat tissue, with numerous peaks *(gyri)* flanked on either side by valleys *(sulci)*. As the brain ages, it changes physically: slowly losing its tall peaks and gaining wider valleys. The brain significantly shrinks and acquires a smoother surface. This age-related loss in brain mass occurs at an earlier age in women than men. Ironically, women begin to lose the wrinkles in their brains at an age when they notice the increasing appearance of wrinkles in their skin!

Fortunately, for every rule, there are exceptions. Many of us have personal stories of eighty- and ninety-year-old relatives and friends whose intellectual capacities do not seem to show any signs of age. Studies have confirmed that the brains of certain individuals do not lose a significant amount of volume. Instead, these brains resemble those of much younger people. This only goes to show that whether on the physical or mental level, the rules of brain aging can and are meant to be broken!

THE AGING OF THE MIND

If somebody stopped you on the street today and asked you to rate your memory, what would you say? Well, if you are a typical person over the age of fifty, you will probably say that it isn't as good as you'd like it to be. Studies have shown that compared to young people, older adults have a greater tendency to rate their memory ability as poor; many of them believe that they forget things in their everyday lives more frequently and perceive their memory as declining rather than remaining stable or improving. Perhaps most significantly, many older adults see age-related memory decline as inevitable and not modifiable by practice and training.[1] The perception that memory and other mental abilities plummet as chronological age rises stems from people's interpretation of their personal episodes of memory lapses. The stereotypical portrayal of forgetful older people by the popular media also helps cultivate this belief.

In reality, many people do not reach the pinnacle of knowledge and intellectual skills until relatively late in life. The minds of people who lead intellectually stimulating lives can even continue to grow and mature well into late adulthood and old age. But how then can we explain the observation of most middle-aged people that they are not able to learn and remember new things as swiftly as they did during their college years? The evolution of certain characteristics of the human mind as we age accounts for this phenomenon. The efficiency and speed by which we learn new information

> ### *Great Minds Don't Necessarily Think Alike*
>
> **A statistical measure of variability demonstrated that compared with their forty-year-old counterparts, the mental test scores of seventy-year-old physicians had 60 percent more variability, and those of seventy-five-year-olds had greater than 100 percent more variability. In other words, as people get older, their mental abilities become less uniform. Rather than becoming more alike and uniformly senile, our minds actually become more *different* the older we get!**

1. Hultsch D, Hertzog C, Dixon RA, Small BJ. *Memory Change in the Aged.* Cambridge: Cambridge University Press, 1998.

peak somewhere between the ages of twenty and thirty years, followed by a plateau period that typically extends several decades. Certainly, this does not mean that people in their thirties and forties cannot learn new concepts and skills; only that it may take them slightly longer to do so compared with when they were in their twenties. Fortunately, the wealth of life experiences, knowledge, and skills that we accumulate with age is more than enough to mitigate the very subtle decline in learning efficiency. In fact, a study of changes in mental speed with age showed that there were seventy-year-olds who surpassed the performance of some people in their twenties. This highlights the remarkable ability of the human mind to adapt to age-related changes by relying on mental skills acquired through experience.

THE HARVARD STUDY

A Harvard University study of more than a thousand aging physicians reported that between the ages of forty and seventy-five years, mental ability can be expected to decline by as much as 20 percent. Upon casual inspection, this appears to be rather disturbing, especially when taken together with other studies showing that average scores on memory tests decline steadily as early as after age twenty-five. But the mental declines with age observed in these highly educated professionals are not as apocalyptic as they may initially seem. The key word here is *average*. This means that while some people suffered a decline of 20 percent or greater, others had a much less precipitous drop in mental function and still others experienced no mental decline at all. If anything, the findings of this study helped shatter the widely held belief that mental capacities decline uniformly with age.

How can we explain the fact that at age seventy-five, some people are playing chess, balancing their checkbooks, and tending their gardens, while others cannot even find the nearest bathroom? This is the million-dollar question that we will answer in the rest of this book. One thing we know for sure: Not all people are destined to suffer a decline in mental capacity simply because of age. Clearly, other factors are at play separating those who are able to keep the mind young from those who begin losing it even before they reach middle age.

RAYS OF HOPE

Many scientific studies have shown that the minds of people age differently. By conscious effort or pure luck, some of us will choose the path that leads to successful brain aging, allowing us to keep our mental capacities intact indefinitely. But some of us might not be so lucky and instead choose the path that leads to memory loss. The clear message of the most recent scientific studies is this: Taking relatively simple steps has the potential of altering the destiny of the mind. If you were presented with the choice, which path would *you* choose?

Chapter 2

Mental Wear and Tear

While many of us know how to drive a car, most of us can only imagine what intricate mechanical operations must occur underneath the hood before a two-ton vehicle can move even a few feet forward. To run smoothly, the vehicle must have good steering, transmission, brake, and fuel systems. A breakdown in any one of these systems will inevitably affect the others and, ultimately, the ability of the car to function effectively as a whole. Note that not all components of the vehicle are equally vulnerable to damage. As time and mileage take their toll, one part may suffer more wear and tear, consequently failing sooner than others. For instance, it is not unusual for the brake pads to wear out before the transmission fails.

Mental aging is sometimes referred to as wear and tear of the mind. One or more of its component abilities may succumb to the effects of time or a certain disease, while others are left relatively preserved. For instance, one person's ability to remember names may decline sooner than her ability to plan and sequence her schedule. And while it takes a physician who specializes in memory problems to figure out why a person has frequent memory lapses (just as it takes an expert mechanic to figure out why an automobile makes a strange noise when it reaches a certain speed), everyone should at least be familiar with the effects of age on these different mental abilities. The reason is that only by breaking down the mind into its component parts can you distinguish areas of relative mental weakness from areas of relative strengths. This is the approach I will take in testing your mind's abilities in the Memory Stress Test section of this book as well as in targeting areas of weaknesses in the memory improvement section.

THE MIND'S COMPONENT PARTS

Like an orchestra made up of many musicians playing different instruments that blend perfectly to produce beautiful music, the human mind is made up of several distinct mental abilities that normally act in synchrony to function as a logical whole. These mental abilities are referred to as the *cognitive domains.* Memory, attention, and language are just some examples of these. Whether remembering a grocery list or interpreting an abstract painting, the performance of any mental task requires the intimate cooperation of two or more of these cognitive domains. Even the most seemingly mundane chore demands the complex interaction of several mental abilities. Consequently, when even a single domain fails, many different functions are affected.

One of the most exciting and controversial areas of brain research explores the differences between memory changes that occur with normal aging and those that are caused by disease, such as Alzheimer's. The changes often overlap. One good way to clarify this issue is to follow large groups of mentally intact people from their youth to old age and note how their mental functions change with time.

Umea, a city in the northern part of Sweden of about a hundred thousand inhabitants, was the site of one of the best-known studies on cognitive aging. This part of the world is a particularly good place to study aging because of the exceptional longevity of the population: Approximately two-thirds of the Swedish population reaches the age of sixty-five. In addition to having long lives, the population of Umea is also rapidly aging. This makes the population even easier to study—we do not need to wait for very long before the signs of mental aging start to emerge. The city is known in Sweden for its abundance of birch trees; *betula* is the Latin word for "birch tree." Thus, over the years this study on human aging has become known as the Betula Study.[1] Participants filled out detailed questionnaires about their social background and habits and underwent extensive memory testing and physical examination, including blood and sensory function tests. The information collected provided a background that made it possible for the researchers to make close observations and conclusions about the aging human mind. The following sections describe the findings of the Betula Study and similar experiments that examined how wear and tear on several of the mind's cognitive domains affect the way we think. These include:

1. *Memory*
2. *Language*
3. *Attention*
4. *Executive function*
5. *Visual abilities*

---

[1]Nilsson L, Markowitsch HJ. *Cognitive Neuroscience of Memory*. Göttingen: Hogrefe & Huber Publishers, 1999.

It is important for us to understand how each of these elements changes as we age. As you explore each, you are likely to identify your own areas of mental weakness that you will want to focus on while applying the information and the exercises presented in this book in your daily life.

Memory

The Betula Study confirmed what people have long suspected: Memory abilities tend to decline with age. The researchers proved this by giving each participant a series of tests that were meant to mimic common tasks performed in everyday life. One test evaluated their ability to recognize faces by showing them sixteen color pictures of faces and the corresponding name for each. They were later asked to pick out the faces of people they had previously seen and to state the name that matched each face picture. Another test involved the ability to recall recently acquired facts. For this, the people studied made-up facts about famous people. An example (which is not part of the test) would be a statement that actress Julia Roberts collects rare books as a hobby. Because this is not a factual statement, it virtually guaranteed that participants were hearing this piece of information for the first time. After a few minutes, they were quizzed on this with the question "What is Julia Roberts's hobby?" Other tests involved

> *Quick Memory Checks*
>
> **Do you remember what you had for dinner two nights ago? How about the eye and hair color of your first date?**

word fluency and comprehension. For example, the volunteers were asked to name all the five-letter words beginning with the letter *m*, or all the professions that begin with the letter *b*, that they could remember within a one-minute time limit. Taken together, the results of the extensive tests confirmed that memory abilities decline with advancing age. The magnitude of decline was neither great nor dramatic but enough to show that in later years, the ability to remember may not be as good as it used to be.

This finding has been confirmed by other studies. The Wechsler Memory Scale is one of the most commonly used sets of tests for memory abilities today. But before it found such widespread popularity, researchers had to establish the normal cutoff or passing score to distinguish normal from abnormal performance. To accomplish this, they administered the same test to large groups of volunteers belonging to different age groups. These included such tests as the ability to recall or recognize stories, words, and faces. The researchers discovered that between the ages of twenty and eighty, there is a decline of 1 to 1.5 in the standard score. Simply put, if someone at age twenty had a memory score that was at the perfectly respectable 85th to 90th percentile range, by age seventy his score would have declined to the 50th percentile. And if someone had a low memory score to begin with—say, the 50th percentile at age twenty—her score could be expected to fall somewhere between the 10th and 15th percentile at age seventy![2]

---

2. Salthouse T. Age-related effects on memory in the context of age-related effects on cognition. In *Lifespan Development of Human Memory*. Cambridge, MA: MIT Press, 2002: 139–158.

Although age certainly played a part in the results of the Betula Study, other factors such as the number of years of education may also have contributed to the differences between the memory performance of the old and the young. In fact, the researchers found that while the youngest participants in the study had an average of fourteen years of education, the oldest in the group had spent only half as many years in school. If the number of years of schooling was taken into consideration in interpreting the results of the word fluency and vocabulary tests, the differences between young and old disappeared. This finding is particularly relevant, because one way that many of us predict our mind's future is by looking at our parents. Since they are the sources of our genes, it is almost intuitive that when we reach their age, we will have very similar mental abilities and disabilities. While logical, this conclusion may not be accurate given the differences in the educational and other opportunities that the baby boomer generation has experienced that their parents did not. These generational differences in education, diet, occupation, and other factors may spell the difference between the frail and forgetful old age of our parents and a healthy and active one for the boomers. But of course, this is only true for those of us who actually take time to learn and practice the right steps in healthy brain aging. Those who do not are bound to commit the same mistakes, such as mental stagnation and poor nutrition, as their parents did. Throughout this book, I will tell you the most important things you should be doing and avoiding to improve your chances at preserving your sharp memory ability. In chapter 11, The Memory Stress Test, you will have a chance to evaluate your verbal and visual memory and to see how they stack up against your other mental abilities.

Language

We often use the expression "It's on the tip of my tongue" when we really mean to say, "It's on the tip of my mind." The mind, and not the tongue, is the real culprit for problems in extracting names from our memory banks. The perception of a faltering ability to remember a name is one of the most common complaints of people as they get older. Many of my patients feel deeply embarrassed when they find the need to stop in midsentence to flex their mental muscle before they can retrieve a familiar name. Names of people and places that used to roll off their tongues suddenly require a significant degree of effort to pluck out from the deepest recesses of their minds.

> *Quick Language Tests*
>
> **Do you remember the complete title of the last movie you saw? How about the name of the kid who sat next to you during algebra class?**

Naming is just a small part of the larger cognitive domain of language or verbal ability. Our mind's language ability encompasses such skills as reading, writing, comprehending, and repeating words or phrases. Compared to other mental functions, verbal abilities generally tend to be resistant to the effects of age. A notable exception to this rule is the naming ability, which is the first verbal ability to decline with age. In fact, by the time they reach their seventieth birthday, most people will experience measurable decreases in their ability to name even common household objects. It is also not uncommon for people with otherwise normal memory to encounter problems in remembering names.

Unfortunately, not all problems in naming are equally innocuous, since this mental function is also the language ability most vulnerable to degenerative brain diseases such as Alzheimer's. The naming problem experienced by a person with a degenerative brain condition typically begins subtly. He may have difficulty in recalling the name of an old friend he hasn't seen for a while, or in remembering the name of a place that he hasn't visited for years. If he tries hard enough and applies considerable mental effort, the name can usually be retrieved from the coffers of his memory bank. But the naming problems of these people do not stop there. As the disease progresses, so does the naming difficulty. People in the moderate to late stages of Alzheimer's may even mistake names of common objects for each other or substitute the purpose or a quality of an object for its name. For instance, they might call a pencil a "writing instrument" or identify candy as "sweet stuff." Some may even make up new words for common objects whose names they have forgotten.

In the Memory Stress Test, I have provided a practical way to test naming ability with the use of common objects found around the house. Certain mental techniques have been shown to be effective in decreasing the mental work required to remember names, places, and even lists of items such as groceries. In chapter 12, The Memory Improvement Program, we will get acquainted with these techniques and learn how to apply them in our everyday lives to keep our language and naming abilities as sharp as possible.

A Test of Attention

Try this simple exercise: Look around you and memorize five things in the room you are in that are colored *red*. Do not read any farther until you have done this.

Attention

Before you read this section, perform the test of attention presented in the sidebar. Have you looked around the room and committed five red objects to memory? Now close your eyes and try to name five things you saw that were colored *blue*. How many did you remember? If you are like most people you will likely be able to name only two or three blue objects. Don't panic; this doesn't mean that there is something wrong with your memory. When you were instructed to look for things that were colored red, your mind simply did not pay any attention to objects that were of a different color. This illustrates the essential role that attention plays in forming new memories. While our eyes can see many images at once, our mind's eye can only focus on one task at a time. You may have already realized this if you ever tried to memorize a phone number, only to lose it after being distracted by another stimulus, such as a co-worker who decided to strike up a conversation. This common experience is completely normal. But for people with an abnormally short attention span (such as children suffering from the condition known as attention deficit disorder or ADD), the mind simply cannot focus on the task at hand even in the absence of strong distractions. While there are certain types of stimuli, such as loud explosions, that can distract even the most attentive person, people with short attention spans are readily distracted by minor stimuli like bright-colored objects, which most of us can easily ignore when focusing on a certain task.

Attention is one of the cognitive domains that can decline as we age. People with attention problems will tend to repeat questions that have already been asked and answered to their satisfaction. They can also forget details of recent conversations or even fail to remember that the conversation ever took place. Some may misplace things because they do not pay attention when they set something down. Poor attention to road conditions and other automobiles causes some older drivers with attention problems to have frequent fender benders. Some studies show that age alone is not enough to cause a person's attention ability to decline. This means that factors other than age must be present to experience attention deficits of sufficient severity to interfere with a person's everyday life. For instance, older people with poor hearing or vision may be wrongly labeled as inattentive. Certain degenerative brain conditions such as Alzheimer's disease can also compromise a person's ability to attend to a task without being distracted. In fact, attention is one of the first mental functions to be affected by the very early stages of Alzheimer's. Because of this, people afflicted with the disease benefit from frequent reminders, redirection, and reorientation until they are able to absorb and comprehend the new information.

Do you think you are forgetting things because you are simply not paying attention to what is going on around you or what other people are saying? In the Memory Stress Test, I will provide you with a simple way to test your attention and concentration abilities that will help you answer this question. In the memory improvement section, I will give you some exercises and practical advice on how you can maximize your ability to mentally focus on the task at hand.

Executive Function

Whenever I find myself in Southern California to attend a conference or give a talk, I take the opportunity to drive to Pasadena to visit my elderly parents. Through the years, I have learned that it is best not to let them know of my coming in advance to avoid having them make unnecessary preparations. This also keeps me from disappointing them in case my tight schedule prevents me from making the forty-five-minute drive from Los Angeles or the two-hour drive from San Diego.

> ### Quick Tests of Executive Function
>
> **Can you talk on the phone while cooking an unfamiliar meal by following the steps in a cookbook? How about typing or writing the lyrics of the national athem while watching a fast-paced program, such as an action film or game show on television?**

These unheralded sojourns invariably lead to two things: a stern admonishment for not giving them enough time to prepare for my visit, and a four-course meal. The surprise visit never deters my father from preparing an elaborate feast in the time that it takes me to walk the dog around the neighborhood. He makes this possible by having the twenty or so ingredients prepared well in advance, in case an unexpected guest decides to drop by. He first places the ingredients on small plates and then strategically lines them up on the kitchen counter. Often, he uses all four burners of the stove to simultaneously cook several dishes. He rapidly and frequently shifts his attention from the wok to the saucepan to the pot then back to the wok, careful not to let any one of them go on the flame too long.

I often use my father's stellar ability to juggle several tasks at one time to explain the mind's executive function ability. *Executive function* refers to the ability to plan and the mental flexibility to shift from one task to another. The term *multi-tasking*, originally used to refer to the ability of the central processing unit (CPU) of a computer to run more than one task at the same time, has become a business buzzword colloquially applied to a person's simultaneous handling of multiple tasks. These days, multitasking is the only way that many people in various demanding professions manage to stay sane when they're insanely busy. It is a mentally demanding and stressful technique that our clinic secretary employs on a regular basis when she answers the phone while banging away at the computer and talking to the doctors and nurses. Multitasking is a real-life acid test of the limits of a person's executive function ability. My father, a retired professional chef, owes his ability to plan, organize, sequence, and seamlessly shift tasks to his mind's robust executive function ability. The great dish he cooks is a testament to his intact mental capacities. But not everyone is so fortunate as he. Executive functions have been shown to decline by age seventy in otherwise normal individuals. People with lower levels of education appear to be particularly vulnerable to this problem. Degenerative conditions such as Alzheimer's have also been shown to cause an even more dramatic decline in executive functions, particularly in shifting from one task to another. In the Memory Stress Test, you will have a chance to test your executive function by performing tasks that require mental flexibility. And in the Memory Improvement Program, you'll learn some exercises that will help you to mentally shift from one task to another.

Visual Abilities

Navigating our way around the increasingly complicated world in which we live is a skill that we must apply every day. The amount of mental work this entails tends to vary widely, depending on our particular life situation. For those of us afflicted with wanderlust, it means having to follow a map to get to the nearest subway station in a foreign city. For the seasoned neurosurgeon, it means gently digging into a person's brain to find a tiny aneurysm. And for people who live a very restricted life, it could be as simple as finding their way from the living room to get to the kitchen.

> *Quick Tests of Visual Ability*
>
> **Can you put the different parts of a furniture or toy together by following the sketches and instructions provided with the product? Do you think you can find your way back home if you follow a map or use familiar landmarks to explore areas of your neighborhood that you have never been to before?**

Visuospatial ability refers to people's capacity to orient themselves and to manipulate objects in space. People who have a defect in this domain could get lost in a familiar environment or encounter difficulty in performing tasks that require spatial orientation such as building a doghouse or crocheting a flower pattern. A common way to test this ability is to ask a person to copy a three-dimensional figure such as a cube. Some studies show that as long as a person's vision is good, the ability to copy a two-dimensional figure is not affected by age. However, the capacity to copy a three-dimensional figure can decline in people over the age of sixty.[3] More practically, this means that a person who is able to perform relatively simple and familiar tasks may not necessarily do as well with a more complicated and unfamiliar one. Degenerative brain conditions cause visual abilities to decline earlier and at a faster rate than can be accounted for by age alone. For instance, people with Alzheimer's disease may do quite well while living in their own homes, but once they are taken away from that familiar environment, they can get hopelessly disoriented. Other age-related factors that are extrinsic to the mind, such as poor visual acuity and hearing ability, may also give rise to difficulty in performing tasks that are visually demanding. In the Memory Stress Test, visual ability will be tested together with executive function. As you will see, these tasks require not only good planning and sequencing abilities but also good visual scanning and spatial orientation.

AGE BE NOT PROUD

Aging of the cognitive domains—including memory, language, attention, executive function, and visual abilities—follows a predictable pattern for most people. However, not everyone follows this pattern. The wide variability in mental

3. Albert MS, Moss M. *Geriatric Neuropsychology.* New York: Guilford Press, 1988. Albert M, Moss M. Neuropsychology of aging: findings in humans and monkeys. In Schneider I, et al. *The Handbook of the Biology of Aging.* San Diego: Academic Press, 1996: 217–233.

capacities of people who are the same age attests to the fact that age is not the ultimate determinant of the mind's demise or survival. Other, more powerful forces are involved in determining the winners of the mental preservation game. One such factor lies within the structure of the brain itself. The human brain has been shown to have a remarkable degree of redundancy. This characteristic prevents the brain function from being compromised even after substantial numbers of brain cells have been lost. The "slack in the system" implies that the remaining brain cells have the capacity to compensate for those that are lost. Whether by the formation of new cells or of new connections among existing brain cells, the overall result of this process is the successful avoidance of any observable changes in mental function with age.

This capacity of the human brain to constantly remodel its architecture is referred to as *brain plasticity*. This ability is strongest during infancy and childhood and gradually declines after the first decade of life. This explains how some young people manage to quickly and completely recover from certain forms of brain damage that the inflexible older brain may not even be able to survive. Fortunately, brain plasticity is never completely lost during old age; a certain degree remains even very late in life.[4] Every one of us, regardless of age, is endowed with brain plasticity that helps keep our mind intact.

Your brain's plasticity, as measured by the amount of its functional reserve, is a critical factor that determines your mind's overall resistance or vulnerability to degenerative diseases such as Alzheimer's. Is there a way to make the brain more plastic? Scientists believe that the human brain builds

---

4. Ball LJ, Birge SJ. Prevention of brain aging and dementia. *Clin Ger Med* 2002:485–503.

up its reserve in two ways.[5] The first is to increase *passive brain reserve*. This is the brain's inherent way to protect itself from the many things that threaten its integrity. Excellent genes, proper nutrition, good social supports, adequate education, and intellectual stimulation all play essential roles in building passive brain reserve. The term *passive* is somewhat misleading, because it implies that a person need not exert any effort to sustain it. This is not true. In fact, passive brain reserve must be actively preserved throughout life by proper environmental, lifestyle, and preventive medical care. If a person does not take care of her brain during her youth, her passive brain reserves are bound to wear thin by the time she reaches middle age.

While passive reserves prevent the brain from harm, the second type of reserve depends on the brain's ability to adapt or compensate when damage does occur. *Active brain reserve* refers to the brain's capacity to activate areas that it does not normally use to take over the functions of areas that have been lost to disease, injury, or normal wear and tear. A brain high in active reserves is considered to be very plastic or flexible. It is able to adapt to damage by tapping unused areas and in so doing, dodges the outward manifestation of the disease. Although any amount of reserve can eventually be overwhelmed by disease, conceptually speaking, people with a high level of active brain reserve will be able to resist disease by accessing multiple unused brain areas to make up for those that are lost.

To ensure that our brains will be able to maintain a healthy amount of buffer against disease, we must take steps to

5. Stern Y. What is cognitive reserve? theory and research application of the reserve concept. *J Int Neuropsych Soc* 2002;8:448–460.

preserve and build it up. Specifically, a good and balanced diet rich in antioxidants, regular exercise, prevention of head trauma, and the proper treatment and control of serious diseases such as heart disease and high blood pressure are all necessary to ensure that we are left with an adequate brain reserve to weather the age-related brain damage that typically occurs in late life. Constantly challenging and stimulating our minds through social engagement, lifelong education, and mental exercises can also enhance active brain reserves. In part 2 of this book, you will discover some of the most promising interventions that can lead to a more plastic brain.

THE HEALTHY MIND: AGELESS OR AGE LESS?

The human mind is a complex and ever-changing entity whose inner workings can be described but never fully fathomed. This complexity makes it almost impossible to predict the exact fate of a person's mind with any degree of accuracy. For sure, among us are a handful of people whose minds are destined to be eternally sharp for simply having won the genetic lottery. But realistically speaking, most of us who will succeed in age-proofing our minds will do so by (consciously or unconsciously) making the right lifestyle choices. As you have learned in this chapter, the vast majority of people are not born with an ageless mind; subtle age-related changes in memory and other mental functions are characteristic of usual aging. However, as I will discuss later, there are simple steps we *can* take to make the mind age less rapidly. Reducing oxidation and inflammation, increasing participation in specific types of mental and physical activities, and other relatively simple interventions have shown great promise for this purpose. Following these steps, which will be outlined in the rest of this book, will tip the survival odds in the mind's favor. While all of us stand to benefit from these interventions, it is particularly crucial for those of us whose minds are deteriorating faster than others to do something about it. How do you know if you fit in this category? Read on. In the next chapter, I will talk about the entity known as MCI, the marker of impending Alzheimer's disease, and answer the most basic questions of how we remember, why we forget, and when we need to worry about our memory.

Chapter 3

MCI and the Prevention of Alzheimer's Disease

"The advantage of a bad memory is that one enjoys several times the same good things for the first time."
—FRIEDRICH NIETZSCHE

When Iris Murdoch, the acclaimed British novelist and philosopher, became forgetful, she initially attributed it to a case of writer's block. This prolific author, who had written more than twenty-six novels during her career, thought that she had simply run out of things to say. But one day, she ventured from the safety of her home in Oxford to visit friends in London and got hopelessly lost. It was then that she realized that something had gone terribly wrong. Iris knew that her memory was slipping away. For several years, her intelligence allowed her to cover up her increasing forgetfulness under a facade of social graces. But eventually, Alzheimer's got hold of her mind so completely that the same woman who'd been proud of her ability to assemble an entire novel in her head before writing the first word became so forgetful that she was not even able to remember the titles of the books she had written.

In an interview she gave when she was still in the early stages of the disease, Iris described Alzheimer's as "a very, very bad quiet place." No disease is more dreaded by the thinking man or woman. Alzheimer's is a fatal and incurable disease that afflicts millions of people around the world. Death may be the dreaded outcome of diseases such as heart disease and cancer, but Alzheimer's takes its victims' lives long before the arrival of death. In fact, people whose lives have been touched by it may even see death as a welcome relief from the physical and emotional devastation it causes. Alzheimer's devastates its victim's life by slowly chipping away at memory, obliterating a lifetime's worth of hopes and dreams, joys and tears, successes and failures.

THE SLIPPERY SLOPE OF MEMORY

Everybody forgets sometimes. The real question is, when does sometimes become too often, and when should we start to be concerned about it? Like Iris Murdoch, most of us consider certain degrees of cognitive error as normal for our particular age or life situation. But as I discussed in the first chapter, age alone cannot be blamed for a memory decline that becomes disruptive to daily life. The frequency and magnitude of the lapses considered *normal* tend to vary subjectively from person to person and from one time to another. Most of us will probably start to worry when we sense memory lapses that are becoming more frequent than the occasional slips of the mind. Still, not many are likely to turn this concern into action until someone we trust and care about, perhaps a spouse or a child, points out a serious incident that simply cannot be ignored.

Part of the challenge in separating the worried well from the heedless demented lies in clarifying the ambiguity of what is considered normal memory. Rather than a specific point on a scale, normal memory capacity for an individual lies somewhere within a relatively wide range. The upper and lower boundaries of this range are determined by such variable factors as age, education, occupation, and native intelligence. This variability makes the absolute boundaries of normal memory moving targets that are not as easily defined as other health measures such as those for blood pressure and weight in proportion to height.

I have observed that people have a tendency to forgive themselves for regular memory lapses with trivial consequences but panic after a single episode of forgetfulness that results in a serious or embarrassing outcome. For instance, they feel that not remembering to pick up milk from the supermarket on the way home is okay, but forgetting to show up for an appointment with an important client or to pick up a child from soccer practice is not. While it is true that the societal consequences of these examples of memory lapses are not comparable, are they truly different from the mind's standpoint?

HOW WE REMEMBER

Human memory works on two different levels: short-term memory and long-term memory. *Short-term memory* refers to information temporarily stored in our brain and remembered by focusing our attention. It is characterized by a limited storage capacity (five to seven bits of information at a time) and a short shelf life (thirty to forty-five seconds). For example, when you look up a number in the phone book, you focus your attention and memorize the number just long enough for your finger to dial it. This information is stored in that part of your brain that houses your short-term memories. This type of memory is quite nebulous, as evidenced by the need to look up the number again if you are distracted. Unless you make a conscious effort to store this number in your long-term memory center, your brain purges the number from your memory banks shortly after punching it in. Thus, if you dial the wrong number and the person on the other line asks you what number you are calling, you have to look up the number again.

In contrast, when you are studying for an examination or memorizing the name of an important person who was just introduced to you, the information is relayed from your short-term memory center to the long-term memory center, allowing you to retain and recall the information at a much later time. For this information to stick to your memory for longer than a few minutes, a process called *consolidation* must occur. *Long-term memory*, therefore, refers to information that you know and can recall. These types of memories are more stable and are less likely to be affected by the early stages of a memory disorder such as Alzheimer's disease. In fact, people who are beginning to have memory difficulty often rely on their long-term memory to compensate for difficulties in short-term memory. This explains why older folks with memory problems are fond of making reference to "the good old days." The information stored here is meant to be available long term, perhaps permanently, though—as we will see later—we may not always be able to recall this information when we need it.

THE TWO MEMORY TYPES

If I asked you to type the names of the last five presidents of the United States on a sheet of paper, I would actually be gathering information on the status of two different memory types. Recalling the names requires one type called *declarative memory*, while remembering how to use the typewriter requires what we call *procedural memory*. Declarative memories are constructed consciously and can be "declared" verbally. Examples of this type of memory include the memorization of facts, such as historical dates or a person's name. Once this type of information is effectively stored in the memory banks, it becomes available for conscious recall at a later date. Because it involves consciously learning new information, it is sometimes referred to as *explicit memory*.

Procedural memory, on the other hand, involves the ability to tune and modify the brain networks that support skilled performance. As the name suggests, it includes memory skills that develop with long-term practice, such as riding a bicycle, playing basketball, and touch typing. These memories are not available for conscious recall and typically involve complex motor skills. It is also sometimes referred to as *implicit memory*. Declarative memories are more vulnerable to the effects of degenerative brain diseases than are procedural memories. This explains why a golfer with Alzheimer's disease may still have a killer swing although he has long forgotten the rules of the game.

Why are these distinctions important? Memory problems can appear in many different forms. Some people may have only short-term memory problems with intact long-term memory ability. Alternatively, others may encounter problems with facts and dates but have no problem playing the piano or crocheting a complicated design. Brain mapping studies have shown that the different levels and types of memory are actually located in distinct parts of the brain. Thus, a disease process that affects one may not necessarily affect the other, giving rise to peculiar patterns and degrees of memory loss that distinguish the several forms and stages of dementia. To understand the process better, let's consider the stages followed by the human mind in the formation of a single memory.

THE HUMAN MEMORY AS A FILE CLERK

One commonly used technique to test short-term, declarative memory is called the *delayed recall task*. This involves the memorization of a list of words, pictures, or even paragraphs and recalling a predetermined minimum number of items after a five- or ten-minute delay. This is considered the most difficult type of memory task because it involves all three stages of memory processing:

1. Encoding
2. Storage
3. Retrieval

Encoding is the first stage of human memory. It is the mind's ability to hold and consolidate information. Information received from the senses is processed and converted into a form that the mind can recognize, much like the way a computer converts information it receives into binary codes. The second stage of memory is *storage*, the ability to hold information over time. This demands that the mind find a logical way to file the information so that it can be located easily when needed. *Retrieval* is the last stage of memory and is the ability to search and access information from the knowledge base. The three stages of memory occur sequentially, and the efficiency of each step is dependent on how well the previous stage was performed.

Consider the memory analogy of the file clerk. When the clerk receives a new file, he organizes it, puts it in a folder, and labels it (encoding). He then opens the file cabinet and finds the right place for it, either alphabetically or by categories (storage). A few months later, when someone asks him for a copy of the file, he opens the file cabinet and retrieves the correct folder (retrieval). The efficient retrieval of the file demands that the clerk perform each step correctly. If he makes a mistake in the very first step by putting the file in the wrong folder or by mislabeling it, he will inevitably store it in the wrong place. Later, when he tries to retrieve the file, he will encounter substantial difficulty and it will take him longer to do so. Similarly, if our minds fail to perform any one of the three stages of memory, the memory task is doomed to fail. For instance, if we are introduced to a new person but our mind is unsuccessful in forming a connection between her name and her appearance, we will find it difficult to remember her name when we see her again.

WHY WE FORGET

The psychological literature is filled with theories that attempt to explain the whys and hows of *normal* forgetting. Although the term may sound like an oxymoron, the fact is, not all forgetting is pathologic. Normal people *do* forget sometimes. Most of the time, we forget things that are trivial, such as our seventh-grade math teacher's name or the title of a song playing on the radio. But sometimes, our mind inadvertently flushes out more important information, like remembering to pick up an anniversary gift or where we left our keys. The societal consequences of our memory's failure do not alter the way we forget. Thus, forgetting to return a book to the library and forgetting to show up for an important meeting involve similar system failures of the mental mechanism.

So why do we forget? The most widely accepted explanations are summarized by the three theories of forgetting:

1. Retrieval
2. Interference
3. Fading

As I explained in our discussion of the three stages of memory, *retrieval* refers to the ability to recall information that has been stored in our long-term memory. Just as we may have difficulty retrieving a computer file if we don't save it in the right folder, we may not be able to retrieve information stored in our long-term memory because it was poorly organized and misfiled at the time of storage. This failure of memory consolidation happens when we become distracted and fail to focus our attention while we are attempting to store the information. Although the information has not disappeared, it has been misplaced and is essentially forgotten. But this seemingly lost information may still be found with the help of memory cues. This explains why asking for the first letter of a name or picking the name out from a list of three different names helps us to recall the name of a person or place more easily.

In contrast, *interference* occurs when there is a conflict between old and new information stored in memory. Due to limited space, new information competes with or even replaces old information for the available space. Thus, a barrage of new information may make it more difficult to recall old information by interfering with its retrieval or by replacing it altogether.

The phenomenon of interference is best illustrated by people who mistakenly call a new acquaintance by the name of a person from their past, whose name may sound similar or who may physically resemble the person they just met. In this scenario, the mind plucks out the wrong item from its storage bin, resulting in an error.

Lastly, we may forget certain bits of information because they have simply faded away. According to the *fading* theory of forgetting, our memory works much like a path in the woods. When we do not use the path for a while, it eventually becomes overgrown and disappears completely. This explains why we may not recall our phone number from a few years back or the words to a song we have not heard for a very long time.

In all probability, all three mechanisms of forgetting—retrieval, interference, and fading—are at work during different times in different people. Whatever the mechanism, the final result is identical: that unsettling feeling we get when we forget something we know we should have remembered. And while it is true that everybody forgets sometimes, not everyone forgets to the same extent or for the same reasons. Our vast and rapidly accumulating scientific knowledge on the preservation of memory and prevention of forgetfulness has made it apparent that it is possible to distinguish normal forgetfulness from that which is not. This is where MCI comes in.

WHAT IS MCI?

At the end of my internship year, I decided to reward myself with the purchase of a new car. I had my heart set on a shiny black sports car on display in a local used-car lot. My friends thought that getting a used car with high mileage and no long-term manufacturer's warranty was foolish, especially considering the harsh winters we get in New England. They tried to convince me to shell out a couple of thousand dollars more and get a brand-new Toyota Camry instead. Sensible as their suggestion may have been, in the end I decided to follow my heart (actually, my stubborn brain). On a hot and humid afternoon in late July, I emptied my bank account and drove my sports car home. The car came with a generous sixty-day money-back warranty, so I rode fearlessly all over the crooked streets of Providence throughout the summer. But before long, fall arrived, and with it came the beginning of my car problems. First the muffler developed a hole and needed to be replaced. The carburetor soon followed, and finally the transmission gave out. My shiny black sports car was a lemon.

By winter, I was holding my breath every time I turned on the ignition, hoping the car would start and that the dreaded CHECK ENGINE light on the dusty dashboard would not be flashing. I decided to ignore the warning light, hoping it would just go away. Instead, the lemon ended up broken down on Interstate 95 during an April Fool's Day snowstorm.

In the simplest sense, mild cognitive impairment (MCI) is the brain's warning light for impending Alzheimer's. This disease, unlike a stroke or a heart attack, does not happen suddenly. It is insidious, taking many years to develop and even longer to become obvious to the casual observer. The progression of the disease and the appearance of symptoms are so slow that it frequently goes undetected until it has progressed to the point that not much can be done about it. MCI represents the transition period between normal memory and dementia. It is the gray zone where normal memory ends and the memory problems of Alzheimer's disease begin. Beyond MCI lies the point of no return, where the slippery slope of memory loss awaits.

THE IMPORTANCE OF MCI

MCI is the stage of Alzheimer's disease that is most amenable to interventions that may delay or even prevent the progression of memory loss. As you read on, you'll hear more about promising prevention strategies. Without treatment, one in two people with MCI will succumb to Alzheimer's disease in just three or four years. Millions of people are now living with MCI without even knowing it, mistakenly believing that their forgetfulness is merely a part of normal aging. We may choose to ignore it, just as I chose to ignore the warning light on my old car, but it is not likely to go away.

The recent discovery of MCI represents a breakthrough in Alzheimer's disease research. A Mayo Clinic study showed that out of a group of a hundred people with normal memory, only one or two a year would develop Alzheimer's disease. In sharp contrast, people who have signs of MCI progress to Alzheimer's disease at the alarmingly rapid rate of up to 15 percent per year.[1] Experts believe that when followed over longer periods of time, between 80 and 90 percent of people with MCI will eventually be diagnosed with dementia. Why do the remaining 10 percent not

> ## The Danger of MCI
>
> **Out of one hundred people who have MCI, fifteen will be diagnosed with Alzheimer's disease within the year. In another two years, fifty out of one hundred people with MCI will progress to Alzheimer's.**

develop Alzheimer's? This is currently the subject of intense investigation. Although the CHECK ENGINE light was designed to let you know that something is wrong with the car, an electrical malfunction or a loose gas cap that has nothing to do with the engine at all may also cause it to come on. Similarly, MCI warns of a potential problem in the mind. Not everyone with MCI will develop Alzheimer's disease, but a significant number of them will. I learned the hard way that ignoring my car's warning light wasn't a wise decision. I could have prevented its eventual breakdown had I taken it to a good mechanic. Ignoring the early signs of MCI is equally foolish. As we will see later in the book, making certain lifestyle changes that can decrease the levels of brain oxidation and inflammation and sustain intellectual activity may be able to alter the course of MCI.

1. Petersen RC, et al. Mild cognitive impairment: clinical characterization and outcome. *Arch Neurol* 1999; 56:303–308.

RECOGNIZING MCI

Estimates show that up to thirty-four out of a hundred older people are currently afflicted with MCI.[2] The majority of people living with this condition are not even aware that they have it, since forgetfulness is a symptom that is all too easy to ignore. I want to emphasize that not everyone who is forgetful necessarily has MCI. Most people who worry about their memory are likely experiencing benign, age-related memory changes. Besides MCI and Alzheimer's disease, there are other causes of forgetfulness, such as anxiety, depression, the excessive use of alcohol or certain drugs, and a variety of physical illnesses. The problem is that a subset of forgetful people already has MCI or very early Alzheimer's disease. Failing to identify them means missing the opportunity for treatment. Ultimately, the question is: Where should we draw the line between normal memory and MCI?

In an effort to identify people with MCI and distinguish them from people with other causes of forgetfulness, researchers put their heads together and developed a set of criteria meant to do just that. These criteria have been shown to be both accurate and reliable. They are based on studies of the natural history of MCI in large groups of people over many years.

For a person to be diagnosed as having MCI, *all* of the following five criteria[3] must be satisfied:

2. Burns A, Zaudig M. Mild cognitive impairment in older people. *Lancet* 2002;260:1963–1965.
3. Petersen RC, et al. Practice parameter: early detection of dementia: mild cognitive impairment (an evidence-based review). Report of the Quality Standards Subcommittee of the American Academy of Neurology. *Neurology* 2001;56:1133–1142.

1. *Memory complaint, preferably corroborated by another person*
2. *Poor performance on memory tests*
3. *Normal performance on tests of other cognitive domains (language, attention, executive function, verbal ability)*
4. *Able to perform normal activities of daily living*
5. *Not demented*

These criteria are fairly straightforward and can be identified even in the doctor's office. Unlike other degenerative diseases, no fancy brain scans or blood tests are necessary to determine if a person qualifies for the diagnosis of MCI. But the low-tech approach to MCI diagnosis does not mean that identifying it is easy. To better understand MCI and how to accurately identify our own risk of succumbing to Alzheimer's disease within the next few years, let's explore each of these criteria further.

1. Memory Complaint

One good way to distinguish normal age-associated forgetfulness from MCI is the degree and frequency of the episodes of forgetfulness. People with MCI tend to have more persistent and troublesome episodes of memory lapses. The memory problems are usually not noticeable to the casual observer and, as Iris Murdoch demonstrated, are easily covered up. The initial identification of MCI relies on the subjective complaint of forgetfulness. The person himself may notice this. But more frequently, a keen spouse, an adult child, or even a close friend is the first to spot the problem. MCI is a condition characterized by memory impairment greater than what we would expect from age alone. The individual with MCI is otherwise normal and able to carry out social and occupational tasks without any obvious problems. In effect, forgetfulness is the only manifestation of this condition.

Although many people feel that they are the best judges of the state of their memory, this is often not true. The problem is that the perception of forgetfulness tends to vary from one person to another. Someone who is scrupulous about her mental prowess and takes pride in her ability to remember may worry when she notices even the slightest change in her memory. On the other hand, someone who leads a fairly simple and routine life may not even notice significant memory changes until somebody else points it out to him. In my memory disorder clinic, I routinely send out an informational letter to new patients before they come in for their appointments. In the letter, I strongly encourage them to ask someone whom they trust and who knows them well to accompany them on their visit. I have learned over the years that a person's view of her own memory abilities is limited. She is always standing too close to the tree to see the forest. I am frequently able to obtain a more objective assessment of the patient's memory from the spouse, adult child, or friend. I have observed that people who do not have a close friend or relative whom they see on a regular basis tend to come in at a later stage of the disease. This is probably because most people who have MCI or even those in the earliest stages of Alzheimer's disease do not necessarily remember what they tend to forget. They need somebody else to point it out to them. In fact, a study showed that a person's subjective memory complaint alone might not be a reliable predictor of an underlying memory problem.[4] This is so because some people tend to over- or underestimate their memory performance. To arrive at the diagnosis of MCI, collateral information is highly desirable.

Studies have shown that the confirmation of a memory complaint by a reliable informant, such as a spouse or an adult child, significantly increases its

> ### Tip
>
> **If you feel that you are getting forgetful, it is advisable to ask people who know you well if they agree with your observation. They may just be waiting for the right opportunity to tell you.**

reliability and accuracy.[5] However, a word of caution is in order here. I have encountered spouses and children who become blinded by their well-intentioned desire to protect their loved one from distress. They conveniently dismiss obvious signs of memory problems as part of growing old. In this case, the person's own account may indeed be more accurate and reliable.

2. Poor Memory Test Performance

From time to time, I receive a call from my friend Bill, a primary care practitioner in the ritzy Beacon Hill area of Boston. Sometimes he calls to invite me to a barbecue with his family at their beach house on Cape Cod. But most of the time, he

4. Riedel-Heller SG, et al. Do memory complaints indicate the presence of cognitive impairment? *Eur Arch Psychiatry Clin Neurosci* 1999;249:197–204.
5. Tierney MC, et al. The prediction of Alzheimer disease: the role of patient and informant perceptions of cognitive deficits. *Arch Neurol* 1996;53:423–427.

calls to get my opinion on a challenging medical case he has
seen in his clinic. He has asked me several times for help in re-
solving a dilemma involving one of his patients who com-
plains of subjective memory problems. To alleviate his most
demanding patients' concerns of possible Alzheimer's disease,
he refers them to my clinic. The typical patient he sends my
way is someone between her late forties and early sixties and
usually of superior intelligence.
Before the discovery of MCI,
I handled this type of situation
by asking Bill some screening
questions before I agreed to see
his patient. I asked him about
the patient's ability to carry out
her work, the stability of her social life, and any manifestation
of unsafe behaviors, such as
getting lost in a strange town
or setting fire to the kitchen by
forgetting to shut off the stove. If the responses to these questions were negative, I assured Bill that this was likely just age-
related memory changes and advised him to simply watch for
the appearance of any of these warning signs of a serious
memory problem. Should those occur, I would be happy to
see his patient. It was my way to keep the Worried Well of
Beacon Hill from overwhelming the capacity of my clinic.

> ### Doctors Don't Always Know Best
>
> **Studies have shown that primary care physicians miss somewhere between 35 and 90 percent of patients with memory problems.**

For decades, a similar sort of exchange occurred between
primary care physicians and memory specialists around the
world. In fact, most of the time, primary care physicians didn't
even speak to anyone about this all-too-common complaint
and simply dismissed the patient with a reassuring pat on
the shoulder. Since the discovery of MCI, I have drastically

changed the way I handle phone calls from Bill and other primary care physicians. In fact, I trust his judgment well enough that when he calls me about a patient, I just ask him to have her schedule an appointment with me. When she comes in, I take a detailed history, perform a thorough neurological exam, and have our neuropsychologist perform a comprehensive set of cognitive tests. One such test involves reading the story of a Boston woman who fell victim to a robbery. A few minutes later, the person will be asked to state what she recalled about the story, with a point given for each element of the paragraph that is remembered correctly. When the scores are tallied up, a person with MCI typically recalls fewer elements of the story than someone of similar age and educational background but with a normal memory. Other ways of testing memory involves memorizing and recalling a list of words or re-creating a complex figure from memory. Examples of some of the tests we use in our clinic will be presented in the Memory Stress Test.

3. Normal Non-Memory Cognitive Domains

When most people think of Alzheimer's disease, problems with remembering come to mind. Although memory is indeed the most prominent mental faculty affected by the disease, other cognitive abilities, such as attention, abstract thinking, executive functions, calculation, and naming abilities, are also affected. One characteristic that distinguishes MCI from Alzheimer's is the relative preservation of these non-memory-related intellectual abilities. This is partly the reason why MCI is a lot more difficult to detect than Alzheimer's. To confirm the presence of MCI, someone must not only recognize that he is becoming forgetful, but also undergo testing by a neuropsychologist to make sure that memory is the only intellectual ability affected and that other intellectual capacities are intact. This criterion of MCI demands that the person achieves normal scores in these tests compared with people of similar age and educational backgrounds.

4. Able to Perform Activities of Daily Living

Activities of daily living (ADLs) is the term used to refer to the basic tasks of everyday life, such as eating, getting in and out of bed, dressing, bathing, and using the toilet. On the other hand, *instrumental activities of daily living (IADLs)* refers to the more complicated functions that allow an individual to live independently. These abilities include grocery shopping, preparing a meal, money management, using the telephone, finding a means of transportation, and taking medications. Those afflicted with MCI are able to perform all of their ADLs and IADLs adequately and independently. If people have problems performing these functions, it suggests that they are in a more advanced stage of memory impairment and are likely to have gone beyond the MCI stage. In fact, one of the required elements for the diagnosis of dementia based on the bible of mental disorders, the fourth edition of the *Diagnostic and Statistical Manual of Mental Disorders (DSM-IV)*, is the presence of significant memory and intellectual impairment that interferes with an individual's social and occupational functioning. It's important to note, though, that the inability to carry out ADLs and IADLs due to a physical disability, such as severe arthritis or blindness, does not necessarily lead to a diagnosis of dementia.

5. Absence of Dementia

This last criterion requires the confirmation that the person in question does not yet have established Alzheimer's disease, but is normal in every aspect except memory. In order to distinguish MCI adequately from Alzheimer's disease and other forms of degenerative memory disorders, researchers have made it clear that people with this condition do *not* yet have dementia. An analogy may make this clearer. If an individual is found to have a significant narrowing of the coronary arteries of the heart due to cholesterol deposits, she is said to have coronary artery disease (CAD). This is medically important because it signifies a higher risk of a heart attack in the future. However, the presence of a blockage alone does not mean that she will surely have a heart attack. Other factors such as the presence of collateral coronary vessels that allow oxygen-rich blood to bypass a critically narrowed coronary artery make it possible for one person to escape a heart attack while dooming another with a similarly narrowed artery—but without collateral vessels—to a massive coronary event. Similarly, MCI signifies a high risk of developing Alzheimer's disease but does not guarantee that the condition will progress further. Other characteristics and factors influence the susceptibility and resistance to Alzheimer's of someone with MCI. One characteristic that could decrease the risk of having a progressive memory problem is a high degree of brain plasticity. I will discuss factors that are thought to contribute to improving brain plasticity in the next section of this book. But first, let's examine the exciting work that is currently being done to detect MCI even before the memory problems commence.

THE EARLY DIAGNOSIS OF MCI

In a perfect world, there would be no MCI and, consequently, no Alzheimer's disease. In a near-perfect world, MCI would be identified very early, and a pill could then be taken to prevent it from turning into Alzheimer's. For now, however, we'll gladly settle for the next best thing.

Plausible evidence points to the early identification of MCI and subsequent intervention as the window of opportunity to delay or even prevent its progression to full-blown Alzheimer's disease. The ideal test for MCI will be safe, fast, inexpensive, and accurate, much like the blood tests we currently have available to detect the presence of high cholesterol or diabetes. Unfortunately, such a test does not exist. However, studies using different techniques of brain imaging have provided very promising results.

PET Scans

In 2002, Charlton Heston single-handedly raised public awareness of Alzheimer's by a few notches when he valiantly announced that he was afflicted with the disease. In a news conference, he explained that the fate of his mind was sealed when a little-known procedure called a PET scan confirmed the diagnosis. This statement triggered a spark of interest in this obscure brain scanning procedure. Heston became such a big fan that he agreed to do a public service announcement touting the use of PET scans in the early diagnosis of Alzheimer's disease.

The *positron-emission tomography (PET) scan* involves the injection of a sugar solution combined with a radioactive substance called a radionuclide into a patient's vein. A few minutes later, when the radioactive tracer has had a chance to diffuse through the bloodstream and bathe the brain, the PET scanner rotates around the patient's head to detect the positrons that are being emitted by the radionuclide. This process reveals the different patterns of sugar utilization by the various areas of the brain and distinguishes between healthy and diseased regions. A healthy brain uses sugar as the primary source of energy in its metabolism and therefore takes up the sugar solution thoroughly, producing a uniform PET scan pattern. Diseased areas of the brain are not able to take up the sugars, producing an irregular pattern. Certain diseases produce specific patterns, depending on which area of the brain is affected. In Alzheimer's disease, the defective areas of the brain are those known to control memory. Therefore, the abnormalities of the brain PET scans of people with this disease become even more pronounced when they are asked to perform memory tasks such as recalling a list of words. Researchers are currently refining this technique in the hope of eventually making it an accurate way to identify the changes that occur in the brains of people with MCI, making early diagnosis and intervention possible.

Functional MRI

Another technique that has the potential to detect MCI is the functional MRI. As the name suggests, the *magnetic resonance imaging (MRI)* uses magnetic fields to create three-dimensional slices of the body with incredible resolution. The MRI has been around for many years, and has been used by physicians around the world to diagnose strokes, brain tumors, multiple sclerosis, and many other brain diseases. The *functional MRI (fMRI)* technique is a relatively recent modification of this technology that allows the visualization not only of the brain's structure but also of its function. The scanner has been modified to detect different patterns of blood flow in the various areas of the brain. An area with low activity will show a correspondingly low level of blood flow. In contrast, an area of the brain that is highly active will have a higher metabolism and blood flow. While functional MRI is free of radiation and generally safe, it is currently used only in highly specialized centers and experimental procedures. People who have metals in their bodies such as shrapnel from an old gunshot wound or an implanted pacemaker cannot undergo this procedure. These people cannot even come near an MRI machine because of the danger generated by the magnetic waves. Despite these limitations, the functional MRI is still considered one of the most promising ways to detect MCI. It does this by revealing the patterns of cerebral blood flow in the different brain regions while the person is performing certain intellectual exercises. Functional MRI may reveal areas of weakness (visualized as decreased blood flow) that may later make the person more susceptible to Alzheimer's disease and other degenerative brain diseases.

Brain Scans and MCI

The technology of brain imaging represents the point of intersection of the fields of quantum physics, computer science, engineering, and medicine. It holds great promise in the early identification of people with MCI and Alzheimer's disease. But as with any new technological advance, the refinement of brain scans will likely take many more years of study before it can be broadly applied to the early detection of MCI. At present, neither PET scans nor functional MRIs have reached acceptable levels of reliability and accuracy to find practical use in memory disorder diagnosis. As scientists are working intensely to develop these techniques further, brain scans are predicted to be the key to preventing the progression of MCI to Alzheimer's by distinguishing forgetfulness due to normal aging from that caused by MCI. Until then, we must rely on the criteria discussed earlier to diagnose MCI and identify those at the greatest risk of succumbing to Alzheimer's disease.

THE PREVENTION OF ALZHEIMER'S DISEASE

Many of us who specialize in the field of memory disorders are convinced that MCI holds the key to eventually finding a way to prevent Alzheimer's disease. Millions of public and private dollars are being funneled into the search for the pill that will stop MCI in its tracks. The National Institutes of Health (NIH) recently launched the Memory Impairment

The Race for an MCI Cure

Governmental agencies are not alone in the race for the discovery of the drug that will delay or prevent the progression of MCI to Alzheimer's disease. MCI has spawned the birth of half a dozen start-up pharmaceutical companies by various research laboratories. Their common goal is to discover the blockbuster drug that will stop memory loss in its tracks. One of the leading drug companies in this venture is Cortex Pharmaceuticals, which is testing its new drug CX516 (brand name Ampalex) for this very purpose. Another drug company, Memory Pharmaceuticals, was cofounded by Nobel laureate and prominent memory researcher Eric Kandel. It is developing its own memory-enhancing compound called MEM 1003. Many other pharmaceutical companies have likewise jumped on the MCI bandwagon, testing different drug classes in various stages of development.

Study, a three-year study designed to investigate the effectiveness of the drug donepezil (brand name Aricept) and vitamin E in delaying or preventing the onset of Alzheimer's disease in people with MCI. Researchers working in this study have been closely following the memory abilities of approximately 720 men and women diagnosed to have MCI in sixty-five centers throughout the United States. The participants, whose ages range from fifty-five to ninety years, are randomly receiving either 10 mg of donepezil, 1,000 international units (IU) of vitamin E, or a placebo pill. They periodically undergo neuropsychological tests of memory and other intellectual abilities to reveal whether vitamin E, donepezil, or both medications can prevent MCI from progressing to Alzheimer's disease. The prospect of stopping the progression of MCI by simply popping a pill a day is so enticing that the National Institute of Mental Health (NIMH) is sponsoring a similar trial examining the safety and efficacy of donepezil and the plant extract *Ginkgo biloba* as cognitive-enhancing agents. Besides standard memory tests, this trial involves the use of the positron-emission tomography brain scan to assess brain activity while performing memory tasks. Together, the results of these U.S.-government-sponsored trials will provide some important answers to the question of the utility of purported memory-enhancing medicines in people who have been identified to be at the highest risk of losing their memory.

The race to find the pill that will prevent Alzheimer's disease has truly begun. Whether the government-funded researchers can prove that inexpensive and widely available medicines, such as vitamin E and ginkgo, are capable of stopping MCI is yet to be determined. The more controversial question is whether one or more of these profit-driven pharmaceutical companies will beat them to it by developing safe, effective, and proprietary memory pills. If they do, bigger issues, such as how much they will charge for it, and whether insurance companies will pay for it, will have to be resolved. The two things we know for certain are that a handsome reward awaits the winner of the MCI race, and that it will likely take several more years before the Food and Drug Administration (FDA) grants its seal of approval to any new drug for MCI. Until then, we have a choice of doing nothing, hoping that Alzheimer's doesn't pay us a visit, or critically examining the vital information we have available to us now and judging what has the greatest potential to save our minds from MCI and Alzheimer's disease.

The recent discovery of MCI has been largely responsible for this shift in focus of memory researchers from merely finding ways to treat the symptoms of Alzheimer's disease to preventing the disease process altogether. Instead of bracing ourselves to put out the fire once it starts, what if we can prevent the fire from starting in the first place? The Chinese word for "crisis" is a combination of the two words *danger* and *opportunity*. MCI is poised to be one of the greatest health crises of our generation but also one of the most promising opportunities for achieving an age-proof mind. If we can find a way to stop MCI in its tracks, Alzheimer's will essentially be eradicated. In the next section, I will discuss the most promising ways to prevent MCI and Alzheimer's disease and explore the intimate relationship between the dangers and opportunities to achieving optimal and lasting health for the human mind.

A CASE IN POINT: THE VISITING PROFESSOR

I spotted them immediately as I entered the office. It was early summer in Boston, and the waiting room was filled with a group of college students waiting for their turn to get their yellow fever and hepatitis shots from the travel clinic nurse whose office was next door. In the far corner of the room sat an older couple. The woman was busy flipping through pages of a thick paperback. The man, dressed in a tweed sport coat, khaki pants, and a red-and-white-striped tie, appeared vaguely familiar to me.

He looked up at me as I walked past him. I gave him a forced smile and a tight nod, in case he expected me to remember him. He didn't smile back but followed me with his eyes until I disappeared behind the glass door that separated the waiting area from the examining rooms. I proceeded to my office at the end of the long hallway lined with examining rooms on either side. On my table, the charts of the patients I was scheduled to see that afternoon were stacked up in a neat pile. At the top of the stack was a thin folder with only an identification sheet and referral letter inside.

A new patient. I quickly scanned the referral letter from the primary physician while walking back to the waiting area, trying to stuff as much information into my brain as I could before I called my new patient into the Memory Clinic.

Dear Dr. Tan:
I would like to refer Mr. William McLean, a 64-year-old Caucasian male, presenting with memory complaints. Mental status score is 29 out of 30. . . .

It took me a fraction of a second to realize where I had seen him before. It was in very different circumstances. Professor William McLean was a distinguished professor at the business school. He was an internationally recognized guru of health care finance. A few years back, I had audited one of his courses, venturing across the Charles River to the B-school's ivy-covered campus every Tuesday and Thursday afternoon to listen to this dynamic, engaging teacher who had a passion for excellence and a short temper in equal measure.

I resumed scanning the two-page referral letter, listing my new patient's mercifully unimpressive medical history and the medications he was taking, but not much else that pertained to his memory complaint. As I reached the glass door to the waiting area, I briefly wondered how I should introduce myself: his former student or his new doctor? Without fully realizing why, I decided on the latter.

"William McLean?" I called out. The elegant woman sitting next to him gave me a subtle wave from the corner of the room. Professor McLean did not appear to notice my call. The chattering of the young people distracted him. Mrs. McLean tapped her husband lightly on the shoulder as she got up from her chair. I purposely did not approach them. Instead, I allowed him to get up from his chair and walk toward me. This gave me a wealth of information even before I had a chance to meet him. I checked his lower-body strength by observing if he was able to get up from the chair without having to push himself up with his hands. I assessed his flexibility as he bent forward to pick up his hat, which had fallen to the floor as he was getting up. I surveyed his balance by watching the stability of his steps as he walked across the room toward me.

"Good to meet you, Mr. and Mrs. McLean," I said as I reached out my hand and introduced myself. "We'll be heading over to the examining room at the end of the hallway."

I searched my former professor's face for any sign of recognition as I shook his hand. I showed them to the examining room, whose wall of green-tinted glass overlooked the medical school quadrangle. Out of the corner of my eye, I noticed Professor McLean looking at me as I took the seat behind the table and began to read the scant medical records in his thin folder.

"Medical informatics!" Professor McLean said unexpectedly. His wife gave him a quizzical and disapproving look.

"Doctor, weren't you in my class a few years ago, giving a presentation on reducing errors in hospitals using computer technology?"

"I didn't think that you would remember," I said bashfully, "but I'm glad you did."

"You see what I'm talking about, Marge?" my old professor said excitedly. "Doctor, can you please do me a personal favor and assure my wife that my memory is just fine so we won't have to waste any more of your time?"

Mrs. McLean rolled her eyes. "Okay, Bill, tell me where you parked the car and we'll be on our way," she said, sounding exasperated.

Like a child chided by his mother, Professor McLean shook his head, folded his arms, and retreated back to his chair.

Mrs. McLean appeared satisfied. "Doctor, I rest my case."

After a few seconds of courteous silence, I asked the couple what specifically had brought them to my clinic.

"He's getting forgetful, Doctor," confided Mrs. McLean.

I asked her to give me specific examples of this problem, and she obliged. Professor McLean sat impatiently in his chair, periodically rolling his eyes and shaking his head. To my relief, I learned that my old professor was doing okay for the most part. He continued to teach the class he had been teaching for the past twenty years, and remained a much-sought-after keynote speaker in national conferences. Mrs. McLean pointed out that while her husband continued to function well in all aspects of his work, she had noticed subtle changes in his memory. They were usually minor things like forgetting to walk the dog or pick up something from the grocery store on the way home, but very atypical for her extremely methodical and intelligent husband.

"There's also this issue of a book he is writing—"

"For God's sake, Mary," interrupted Professor McLean, "you know damn well that I've just been too busy to finish that book."

"Honey, I know you're busy, but you've spent almost every weekend working on that book for the past two years." She hesitated for a moment before turning to me.

"Doctor, the book editor sent back the manuscripts twice because . . . well, because it just wasn't right."

I was familiar with Professor McLean's many books on the health care market economy. He must have published at least ten best-selling books in his career. I had the pleasure of reading one of his earlier books on the restructuring of the American health care system.

"That book editor is a moron. I'm deliberately spending more time writing this one because realistically it will likely be my last one," he said through clenched teeth. "Besides, I'm not getting younger, you know. Doctor, how old do people think I am, twenty-five?"

I proceeded to ask him some general questions that tested his long-term memories and general fund of knowledge. Having read his biography in the alumni magazine a few years back, I knew most of the answers to my questions. I warned him that these questions were very basic, ones that we asked all comers to our clinic—everyone from a rocket science professor at MIT to an assembly-line worker at a factory in South Boston. I told him I hoped he would not be insulted.

"When and where were you born?"

"Where did you go to school and how far did you go?"

"How many children do you have, and what are their names?"

I wished I were asking him something less mundane, like what he thought about the global market economy, or the feasibility of universal health care in the United States. But I asked the standard questions while shouting the answers in my head, hoping that he would hear me. Losing such genius to Alzheimer's would be a tragedy—not only to his family but also to the world.

To my satisfaction and relief, he answered all my standard questions without a hint of difficulty or hesitation. When I asked him about his family, he even gave me the names and ages of each of his eight grandchildren, with a sense of pride I had never seen in my old professor before.

"For this part of the examination, I will ask you to remember four unrelated words. Please try to remember them, as I will ask you to repeat them to me in a few minutes."

Professor McLean nodded. His wife took a deep breath and held it in.

"The words are *freedom, brown, grape,* and *south.* Can you repeat them to me just to make sure you heard them correctly?"

He repeated the words, and we moved on to the other tasks that tested his attention, verbal skills, abstract thinking, judgment, and problem-solving abilities. Everything appeared satisfactory, and from the look of amusement in his face, my patient knew he was doing well.

"Everything looks good," I said with a smile. "Now, if you can just tell me those words I asked you to remember a few minutes ago, we'll be done."

"Sure, Doctor, they are *brown ... freedom ... grape ...* and ... ." He stared at the bare white ceiling as if the words were written there.

After about thirty seconds, Professor McLean took his eyes off the ceiling and asked, "Can you give me a clue?"

"Where did we go for vacation last summer?" Mrs. McLean said before I could stop her.

"South Africa. Oh yes, *south* is the last word."

"I'm sorry, Doctor, I just couldn't help myself," Mrs. McLean apologized after she sensed my disapproval of her interference with the examination. "But this is what I don't understand. How could he remember all those things you asked him and not remember that little word from twenty minutes ago?"

After I gave them a brief explanation of the differences between short- and long-term memory, I asked Professor McLean whether he'd be willing to undergo a neuropsychological examination. I told him that this would paint a more detailed picture of his mind's strengths and weaknesses and would give us a better idea of how his memory was really doing. He came back a couple of weeks later. The neuropsychological test confirmed what I had feared: My old professor had isolated memory impairment, performing at the lowest 10th percentile for his age and educational background. An MRI of the brain showed no abnormality except for age-related decrease in brain size. His blood tests for thyroid function, vitamin B_{12} and folic acid levels, blood counts, and metabolic profiles all came back within normal limits. Professor McLean was suffering from MCI.

The couple confessed that they had never heard of MCI, and they asked whether it was just another term for Alzheimer's disease. I assured them that the professor did *not* have Alzheimer's, but his MCI greatly increased his risk for getting it within the next few years. I knew that Professor McLean was interested to know what he could do about it, so

I told them that the same processes that have been implicated in causing Alzheimer's are likely to also be responsible for the progression of MCI. In the next section, I will discuss some of these processes and what scientific research has revealed about interventions that may halt MCI's progression and even—if started early enough—prevent it altogether.

PART II

Saving Your Mind

Now that we have a good understanding of how the brain works, how it ages, and why memory loss occurs in some people but not in others, let's talk about the latest research on how vitamins, diet, and physical and mental exercise can help prevent memory loss. We'll also examine the fascinating roles of brain oxidation, inflammation, and estrogen supplementation in the prevention of Alzheimer's disease.

In the following chapters, you'll learn what steps you should be taking now to preserve your mind and keep memory loss at bay. I'll help you find answers to such questions as: *What vitamins should I be taking? Can estrogen replacement therapy prevent Alzheimer's disease? Are plant estrogens (phytoestrogens) useful in keeping my mind sharp? What types of exercise are good for my body and mind?*

Read on to learn the answers to these and other important questions about how to make your mind last a lifetime.

Chapter 4

Oxygen Damage and the Brain: To E or Not to E?

"Part of the secret of a success in life is to eat what you like and let the food fight it out inside."

—MARK TWAIN

While the brain is arguably the most important human organ, it is certainly not the largest. Surprisingly, that distinction is held by the skin, which accounts for about 16 percent of the body weight and covers an area of about twenty-two square feet. The average human brain represents a mere 2 percent of the total body weight. However, it preferentially receives 20 percent of the body's blood supply and consumes 20 percent of the total oxygen. The brain's abundant blood supply brings with it the vital oxygen and nutrients that its cells need to survive while taking away harmful carbon dioxide and other toxic by-products of metabolism. If for some reason the flow of blood and oxygen to the brain is abruptly cut off, it will lose its ability to produce the energy needed to perform its functions and protect itself from damage.

The serious consequences of cutting off the brain's blood and oxygen supply, even for just a few minutes, is seen most vividly in the devastating loss of neurological and intellectual function in people who have had a stroke. In its classic form, a stroke leaves a person paralyzed on one side, unable to speak clearly, and bound to a wheelchair. But not all types of stroke are so dramatic. The symptoms of smaller strokes can be subtler, manifesting as occasional forgetfulness that could even mimic MCI and early Alzheimer's disease. In fact, stroke is the second most common cause of memory problems in the Western world, ranking behind only Alzheimer's disease. In certain parts of the world where diabetes, high blood pressure, and other conditions that predispose to strokes are not adequately treated, they have surpassed Alzheimer's as the leading cause of dementia. *Vascular dementia* is the term used to describe forgetfulness caused by one massive stroke or by several small ones that strategically knock out important brain centers involved in storing or relaying information. This type of memory disorder does not always affect the same part of the brain as does Alzheimer's, but the memory loss may present itself similarly, making distinction between the two types of memory loss difficult.

THE DOUBLE EDGE OF OXYGEN

Vital as oxygen is to the function of the body, from the standpoint of brain health, it is a double-edged sword. Scientists who have examined the brains of people who died of Alzheimer's disease discovered that certain forms of oxygen are actually harmful to the brain. *Oxidation* is the process by which the body's cells burn calories from food by adding oxygen to produce energy. But besides useful energy, this process also produces undesirable by-products called *oxygen free radicals*. These are unstable molecules generated during normal oxidation reactions. This toxic form of oxygen damages and kills the cells that it comes in contact with. Fortunately, your body has a built-in defense mechanism to protect your brain from these toxic by-products. *Antioxidants* are naturally occurring substances that protect the body from oxygen free radicals. Compared with other organs, the brain is particularly susceptible to oxygen damage because of the unhealthy combination of a rich oxygen supply, a fast metabolic rate, and a relatively low level of antioxidants. Brain cells are also inherently more sensitive to oxygen damage.[1] All these factors combine to make the brain the primary target for toxic oxygen damage.

From Alzheimer's to Parkinson's, brain scientists have blamed oxygen damage for its role in the genesis of several age-related degenerative brain diseases. They believe that these conditions become more common with advancing age due to the cumulative amounts of oxygen damage over several decades. To prove their point, they have shown that people whose blood contains high oxidation and low antioxidant levels were at increased risk of a memory decline.[2] Further evidence of the link between oxygen damage and Alzheimer's can be seen directly in the brains of people who died of the disease. Under a microscope, their brains are seen to be riddled with abnormal protein structures called *amyloid*

---

1. Behl C. Amyloid B-protein toxicity and oxidative stress in Alzheimer's disease. *Cell Tiss Res* 1997;290:471–480.
2. Berr C, Balansard B, Arnaud J, Rousse AM, Alperovitsh A. Cognitive decline is associated with systemic oxidative stress. The EVA study. *J Am Ger Soc* 2000;48:1285–1291.

plaques, which are believed to be responsible for the brain cell death that eventually gives rise to the forgetfulness of Alzheimer's. For years, researchers sought to find out the mechanism by which the plaques cause brain cells to die. Through a lucky break, they discovered that around these structures are high concentrations of oxygen free radicals. This led them to conclude that these toxic forms of oxygen may be directly responsible.

THE OXYGEN SCAVENGERS

To function optimally, the brain must maintain the delicate balance between oxygen free radical formation and its neutralization by antioxidants. *Oxidative stress* is the term used to describe this dangerous imbalance. Low levels of oxidative stress and an abundant supply of antioxidants characterize the healthy brain. Many of the brain's antioxidants are familiar to most people: the naturally occurring vitamin C (ascorbate), vitamin E (tocopherol), and vitamin A (carotenoids). Like soldiers at war, these vitamins continuously scour the brain, searching out and neutralizing oxygen radicals. These potent and protective vitamins are abundant in many types of foods and are widely available as inexpensive nutritional supplements. Controlling the amount of oxygen radicals generated by our brains is not easy. Thus, researchers wondered whether the solution to the brain oxidation problem is simply raising the antioxidant concentration in our brains by including more of them in our diet. They asked: Can taking more vitamin E a day tip the oxygen balance in our mind's favor and keep Alzheimer's at bay?

VITAMIN E TO TREAT ALZHEIMER'S DISEASE

Of all the antioxidants, vitamin E deserves the distinction of being the most studied vitamin for the treatment and prevention of Alzheimer's disease. Vitamin E is known as a "chain-breaking" antioxidant because it acts by disrupting the chain reaction of events that starts with the generation of the oxygen free radical and leads to brain cell death.[3] Normal concentrations of vitamin E in the blood range from 11.6 to 30.8 μmol/L (micromoles per liter).[4]

People afflicted with Alzheimer's disease have decreased blood and brain levels of vitamin E. This relative deficiency may play a crucial role in the development and progression of memory problems in susceptible individuals.

The effectiveness of vitamin E in improving and preserving memory and intellectual performance was first shown in studies using aged animals.[5] When aging rats were given vitamin E supplements, they were better able to find their way around a complicated maze than those that did not receive the supplements. But the link between vitamin E and memory does not stop there. Several trials using vitamin E as treatment for people with established Alzheimer's disease have also shown promising results. The Alzheimer's Disease Cooperative Study of vitamin E as a treatment for people with Alzheimer's disease is the largest and most prominent study of its kind.

3. Halliwell B, Gutteridge JMC. *Free Radicals in Biology and Medicine,* 2nd ed. Oxford: Oxford University Press, 1989.
4. Meydani M. Vitamin E. *Lancet* 1995;345:170–175.
5. Ichitani Y, Okaichi H, Yoshikawa T, Ibata Y. Learning behaviour in chronic vitamin E-deficient and supplemented rats: radial arm maze learning and passive avoidance response. *Behav Brain Res* 1992;51:157–164.

Researchers found that compared with those who did not take vitamin E, people with Alzheimer's who regularly took a high dose of vitamin E had slower rates of decline in functional abilities and of nursing home placement.[6] Unfortunately, the researchers found that taking vitamin E had no demonstrable effect on memory test performance in people with established Alzheimer's. While a bit disappointing, this finding was not entirely surprising given what is known about the process by which oxygen free radicals destroy brain cells. That is, antioxidants can protect the brain cells from further oxygen radical damage, but it cannot resurrect brain cells that have already perished. This study simply reinforced the logical conclusion that vitamin E is effective in slowing the rate of progression of functional decline associated with Alzheimer's disease, but it is not effective in reversing the associated memory loss. Note that the very high doses of vitamin E (2,000 international units a day) used by this trial are not recommended for most people because of a tendency to increase the risk of bleeding.

FOOD FOR THOUGHT

Alzheimer's disease does not happen overnight. It takes many years to develop; the appearance of the first sign of a memory problem signals a disease process that has gone undetected for a very long time. The unfortunate reality is that once Alzheimer's develops a strong foothold on your brain, it becomes almost impossible to loosen its grip. As with many

6. Sano M, Ernesto C, Thomas RG, et al. A controlled trial of selegiline, alpha-tocopherol, or both as treatment for Alzheimer's disease. The Alzheimer's Disease Cooperative Study. N Engl J Med 1997;336;1216–1222.

other diseases, medicines can help alleviate the symptoms, but the disease itself cannot be cured.

For a slowly progressive but incurable disease such as Alzheimer's, prevention is much more realistic than finding the elusive cure. At the nexus of prevention efforts for memory problems as well as other age-related diseases such as coronary heart disease are vitamin E and other antioxidants. In a study of more than five thousand men and women ages fifty-five and older who were living in the Netherlands, researchers found that people who consumed more than 15.5 mg per day of vitamin E in their diet had a 43 percent decrease in the risk of developing Alzheimer's disease.[7] This effect was not limited to vitamin E, but was also observed with other antioxidants. Those who took 133 mg or more per day of vitamin C or greater than 1.67 mg per day of beta-carotene (vitamin A) in their diet also enjoyed a reduction of their risk for Alzheimer's. Interestingly, cigarette smokers derived the greatest memory-saving benefit from high intakes of antioxidants, over and above that of nonsmokers.

The mysterious link between vitamin E and Alzheimer's sparked the interest of American researchers from the Chicago Health and Aging Project, who were studying a large group of people living in three contiguous neighborhoods on the South Side of Chicago. They examined the differences in patterns of vitamin E intake from food and supplements of these Midwesterners and found that people who took more than 10.4 IU per day of vitamin E in the form of food enjoyed a 70 percent reduction in the risk of Alzheimer's compared with people whose intakes of the vitamin were less than

7. Engelhart MJ, Geerlings MI, Ruitenberg A, et al. Dietary intake of antioxidants and risk of Alzheimer's disease. *J Am Med Assoc* 2002;287:3223–3229.

7 IU per day.[8] People who had high vitamin E intakes also had a slower rate of age-related decline in their memory and other intellectual functions. One exception to this encouraging finding was people with a known genetic predisposition (ApoE4 allele) to developing Alzheimer's disease. This group did not experience any significant risk reduction even if they took lots of vitamin E, suggesting that not everyone who takes antioxidants will escape the disease.

Note that both the Dutch and American studies only demonstrated the beneficial effects of vitamin-E-rich foods, not the form found in supplements. In fact, when researchers from both of these studies examined the effect of regular intake of vitamin E supplements, they found that this was not protective against Alzheimer's disease. One possible explanation for this is that some study participants may not have taken the dietary supplements long enough to derive benefit from them. However, there may also be a more fundamental explanation: The forms of vitamin E found in supplements and those found naturally in food are *not* identical. Vitamin E found in food is primarily the *gamma-tocopherol* form, which has a chemical composition distinct from the *alpha-tocopherol* form of vitamin E found in most supplement pills. Another possible explanation for the lack of prevention benefit from vitamin E supplements is the presence of a yet-to-be-identified substance or nutrient found in antioxidant-rich foods that is really responsible for its protective effect against Alzheimer's.

A more recent study suggests that while vitamin E supplements taken alone may not be effective in preventing Alz-

8. Morris MC, Evans DA, Bienias JL, et al. Dietary intake of antioxidant nutrients and the risk of incident Alzheimer's disease in a biracial community. *J Am Med Assoc* 2002;287:3230–3237.

heimer's, taking them along with a vitamin C supplement may be.[9] The researchers found that taking either one of the two supplements alone or taking only low doses of both vitamins in a multivitamin supplement did not offer any protective effect. When taken together, however, the two antioxidants offered protection against the development of memory problems.

HOW MUCH *E* IS *E*NOUGH?

At present, nobody knows exactly how much vitamin E is needed to protect our brains from Alzheimer's disease. While higher concentrations of the vitamin can be achieved by taking dietary supplements than through food alone, this doesn't mean that vitamin supplements are better than vitamin-E-rich foods. In fact, consuming high amounts of vitamin-E-rich foods has been shown to protect against Alzheimer's, suggesting that lesser amounts of natural vitamin E may be equivalent or perhaps even more effective than higher doses of the pill form.

But people who are unable to feast on antioxidant-rich foods on a regular basis will be glad to know that taking dietary supplements has been shown to increase the concentration of vitamin E in the brain.[10] Vitamin E pills are relatively inexpensive and safe dietary supplements. The main complication associated with these preparations is an increased risk of bleeding when taken at very high doses, such as the 2,000

9. Zandi PP, Anthony JC, Khachaturian AS, et al. Reduced risk of Alzheimer's disease in users of antioxidant vitamin supplements: the Cache County Study. *Arch Neurol* 2004;61:82–88.
10. Pillai SR, Traber MG, Steiss JE, Kayden HJ, Cox NR. Alpha-tocopherol concentrations of the nervous system and selected tissues of adult dogs fed three levels of vitamin E. *Lipids* 1993;28:1101–1105.

IU dose used in some clinical trials. In general, taking vitamin E supplements at a dose of 400 to 800 IU a day combined with a multivitamin supplement is safe except for people who have bleeding problems or who are taking blood thinners or anticoagulants. Take note, however, that a recent study suggests that taking high-dose vitamin E (400 IU or more) may be harmful.[11] Still, many knowledgeable people who are unable or unwilling to modify their diets to include healthy portions of fruits and vegetables packed with vitamin E and other oxidants opt to take vitamin E supplements instead. Given the current information we have about this vitamin and brain aging, this approach may not be a bad idea.

Foods Rich in Vitamin E

- **Broccoli**
- **Carrots**
- **Kale**
- **Grapes**
- **Onions**
- **Sweet potatoes**
- **Blueberries**
- **Spinach**
- **Oranges**

Some healthy recipe suggestions that are both low in calories and packed with antioxidants are provided in appendix A.

TO E OR NOT TO E?

This is the question on the minds of many people, from doctors to researchers to laypeople. An informal poll of medical professionals and scientists attending an Alzheimer's disease conference revealed that more than half of the attendees admitted taking vitamin E supplements regularly. Many physicians and nurses are now loading

11. Miller III ER, Pastor-Barriuso R, Dalal D, et al. Meta-Analysis: High-dosage vitamin E supplementation may increase all-cause mortality. *Ann Intern Med* 2004;142.

up on vitamin-E-rich foods and supplements with the hope that it will protect their minds from dementia. Hands down, the best and safest way to increase vitamin E stores is by taking it in its naturally occurring form. In fact, many foods that are rich in vitamin E offer the added benefit of also being packed with other potentially brain-protecting antioxidants such as vitamin C and beta-carotene.

Aluminum and Alzheimer's

I've known Catherine for more than ten years. She was the supervising resident of the pediatrics clerkship during my third year of medical school. Although we eventually started our respective practices in the Boston area, I didn't see Catherine for several years after I graduated. Two years ago, she accompanied her father, a retired engineer, who had become increasingly forgetful, to my memory clinic. It had come to the point that he had difficulty recognizing grandchildren who gathered around the table for Thanksgiving dinner. After I had a chance to speak with him and perform some memory tests, I realized that his situation did not look good. It broke my heart to have to tell him and his daughter that he had Alzheimer's disease. But both Catherine and her father seemed to take the serious diagnosis remarkably well.

Not long after the visit, Catherine called me to get my opinion on a study she had read about in a medical journal that found a link between the ingestion of minute amounts of metals over many years and memory loss. Concerned about protecting herself and her

(continued)

family from succumbing to Alzheimer's, Catherine said: "I've already stopped drinking soda from aluminum cans. I wonder if there's anything else my family and I should be doing?"

I paused and made sure I had heard her right. I recognized that somehow, Catherine had been misled into believing that aluminum could cause Alzheimer's, and further that refraining from drinking soda from aluminum cans could prevent it.

Aluminum gained notoriety as a suspected cause of Alzheimer's disease in the late 1970s. This began when researchers discovered that compared with the brains of normal people, the brains of people with Alzheimer's have higher concentrations of aluminum. Further evidence that appeared to support this contention came from a study showing that high concentrations of aluminum in the drinking water can increase a population's risk for developing Alzheimer's. Though the belief is not entirely baseless, more than thirty years had passed since it was first proposed and yet no conclusive study had proven that aluminum by itself causes memory problems.

Despite the lack of good evidence, one reason for the continuing credibility of the theory of aluminum as a potential cause of Alzheimer's is its known ability to facilitate the formation of harmful oxygen free radicals. But this characteristic is not exclusive to aluminum. Other metals such as iron, mercury, copper, and zinc are also capable of generating this bad form of oxygen. This ability, and the fact that they have been found in the brains of people with Alzheimer's disease, sustain the rumors that aluminum causes brain degeneration. Eliminating aluminum and other metals from our body is next to impossible. However, there is no shortage of alternative medicine interventions that claim to "treat" or "prevent" Alzheimer's disease by reducing the aluminum content of the brain. One of the more popular interventions is *aluminum chelation therapy,* a process that uses chemicals to extract aluminum and other heavy metals from the body. This questionable, expensive, and potentially dangerous procedure has attracted many families who are desperate to try anything that promises to bring back their loved one. Thus far, the removal of aluminum from the brain has cured no one.

So should we now throw away our aluminum pots and pans and stop drinking soda from aluminum cans? The answer is a resounding *no!* In the process of searching for the true culprit and cure for any disease, it is not unusual to encounter countless things that may initially appear to be *the* cause. Frequently, these circumstantially suspicious agents are later found to be unrelated to the disease. Based on current evidence, I believe that aluminum is one such agent. While it is highly unlikely that aluminum will ever be shown to cause Alzheimer's, we do know that the true culprit will likely be related to the generation of oxygen free radicals. Therefore, increasing our daily antioxidant intake may be our best bet in counteracting any deleterious effects of excessive aluminum on the brain. [Abd el-Fattah AA, al-Yousef HM, al-Bekairi AM, al-Sawaf HA. Vitamin E protects the brain against oxidative injury stimulated by excessive aluminum intake. *Biochem Molec Biol Int* 1998;46:1175–1180.]

Chapter 5

Inflammation and the Brain

*"By the time you're eighty years old you've learned everything.
You only have to remember it."*

—George Burns

Have you ever experienced the excruciating pain of an ankle sprain from a sports injury? How about the swelling of an arthritic joint? Most of us have had a personal encounter with inflammation at some point in our lives. Inflammation is the body's classic reaction to injury or disease. When we hear of something as being inflamed, we frequently conjure up a picture of a body part that is swollen, red, hot to the touch, and often painful. The stubborn pimple that won't seem to go away, the throbbing ache and swelling of an infected tooth, and the disfiguring swelling of a black eye are just some examples of inflammation at work.

Though many consider inflammation as little more than a nuisance, in reality it serves a real and very important purpose. Inflammation is the body's way of preserving its integrity in times of threat or trouble. Through this process, it is able to conquer foreign invaders, repair and rebuild damaged body parts, and alert us to a problem that needs to be taken care of before it gets any worse.

Inflammation begins when a body part or organ is injured. It sends an SOS signal to the immune system, asking it to send in reinforcements in the form of white blood cells. White blood cells are equipped with potent chemicals that can contain the damage, neutralize the bacterial and viral invaders, and summon repair cells to start rebuilding the area. When the situation is resolved, the inflammation process slowly winds down and the white blood cells return to a resting but vigilant state.

INFLAMMATION AND ALZHEIMER'S DISEASE

Ever since the first case of Alzheimer's disease was identified, scientists have closely looked at the brains of people who died of the disease in search of clues that will reveal its true cause. The brains of people with Alzheimer's are studded with abnormal proteins called amyloid plaques. Scientists suspected that these peculiar structures held the secret to the cause (and possibly the cure) for Alzheimer's. Like crime scene investigators, they meticulously pored over the microscopic, spherical structures and the surrounding areas of damaged brain tissues. They discovered that around the plaques are high concentrations of toxic oxygen free radicals, which identified oxidation as a potential cause of the disease. But in addition, the scientists also found *microglial cells,* the brain's equivalent of the white blood cells of the immune system. This suggests that in some way, the immune system plays a role in Alzheimer's

The Immune System and Inflammation

The immune system, with its ability to trigger inflammation at a moment's notice, is an incredibly potent defense mechanism. Unfortunately, it is neither always accurate nor precise in locating its target. In a condition called an *autoimmune disorder,* the immune system mistakes the very organs and tissues that it is meant to protect for foreign invaders that must be destroyed. It summons the white blood cells to destroy organs that are perfectly healthy, resulting in widespread inflammation that frequently leads to devastating consequences. Diseases such as rheumatoid arthritis and lupus are caused by this failure of the immune and inflammatory systems. The rejection of a transplanted heart or kidney has a similar cause. Once a mistake in identifying a target has occurred, it is almost impossible to correct. The only effective treatment for people with autoimmune diseases seem to be powerful drugs that suppress the immune system and anti-inflammatory medications that stop wayward chemical reactions from damaging healthy cells and tissues.

disease. Brain scientists believe that the immune system becomes confused and orders the microglial cells to attack and destroy healthy brain cells. Mistaking its own memory cells for foreign invaders, the brain attacks itself by initiating the inflammatory cascade that destroys its cells and eventually leads to Alzheimer's disease. Proponents of this theory believe that taking anti-inflammatory medicines before too many brain cells are destroyed can interrupt this cascade and prevent Alzheimer's from developing. If this is true, suppressing inflammation has the potential of stopping the progression of the disease. But can doing something as simple as swallowing an ibuprofen tablet a day derail the runaway train speeding toward forgetfulness? To help answer this question, scientists turned to the experience of a group of aging Americans.

INFLAMMATION AND AGING UNDER A MICROSCOPE

In 1958, several researchers from the Baltimore, Maryland, area got together to begin a landmark study on aging. The lofty goals of the study included the gargantuan task of unraveling the mystery of how biology and behavior change as people get older. Starting with only a few male volunteers, the Baltimore Longitudinal Study on Aging (BLSA) has grown to include more than twelve hundred men and women ranging in age from their early twenties to their late nineties. It is now the longest-running study on human aging. Every two years, these volunteers undergo two and a half days of extensive interviews and testing. Through this process, the researchers hope to identify the changes that normally occur with age and to distinguish them from those caused by disease. The research protocol of the BLSA is so comprehensive that the participants are sometimes described as "aging under the microscope." In addition to the numerous blood tests and other procedures, the volunteers have been tested for their mental health, including memory, attention, problem-solving abilities, and behavior during each visit. The wealth of information that has been collected over the years provides a unique opportunity to identify

The Dutch Study

Researchers from the Netherlands followed nearly seven thousand residents of the town of Rotterdam to explore the controversial association between anti-inflammatory medications and Alzheimer's disease. They found an even greater risk reduction than that uncovered by the BLSA. Individuals in this study who took these medicines for more than two years had an 80 percent decrease in their risk of developing Alzheimer's disease. But unlike the results of the BLSA, those who took anti-inflammatory medications for less than two years did not derive any benefit in terms of brain protection.

the characteristics that make people vulnerable to certain diseases as well as those that can protect them.

The role of inflammation in the development of Alzheimer's disease is one of the main mysteries of aging that the BLSA researchers sought to unravel. At their disposal were the medical records of more than a thousand aging people, some of whom had already developed Alzheimer's. The hypothesis was fairly simple: If the association between inflammation and Alzheimer's is real, people who regularly took anti-inflammatory medicines such as ibuprofen would be protected from developing the disease. The researchers sifted through piles of medical records first to identify people who took anti-inflammatory medications regularly for arthritis and other conditions, and later to determine the fate of their minds. What the BLSA researchers found was nothing less than astounding. People who regularly took anti-inflammatory medications for at least two years were 60 percent less likely to develop Alzheimer's disease. Those who took these medications for shorter time periods derived more modest benefits: Taking anti-inflammatories for less than two years decreased the risk by only 35 percent. Further, not all over-the-counter pain relievers showed a strong protective effect against Alzheimer's. Aspirin, which has a weaker anti-inflammatory effect than ibuprofen, bestowed its users only a 25 percent risk reduction, while acetaminophen (Tylenol), an effective pain reliever that is devoid of any anti-inflammatory effect, offered no benefit at all.[1]

Since the results of the BLSA study came out, other population-based studies from the Mayo Clinic,[2] the Netherlands,[3] Cache County, Utah,[4] and about twenty other studies have confirmed that long-term use of anti-inflammatory medicines has the potential of lowering the risk of developing Alzheimer's disease.

Together, the results of these studies point to the usefulness of ibuprofen and similar anti-inflammatory drugs as a potential preventive measure against memory problems. The caveat is that only those who took these medicines regularly for a period of two or more years before the onset of the disease appeared to derive a significant amount of brain protection. Moreover, not everyone can tolerate the gastrointestinal and other side effects of anti-inflammatory medications.

1. Stewart WF, Kawas C, Corrada M, Metter EJ. Risk of Alzheimer's disease and duration of NSAID use. *Neurol* 1997;48(3):626–632.
2. Beard CM, Waring SC, O'Brien PC, Kurland LT, Kokmen E. Nonsteroidal anti-inflammatory drug use and Alzheimer's disease: a case-control study in Rochester, Minnesota, 1980 through 1984. *Mayo Clinic Proc* 1998;73(10):951–955.
3. Veld BA, Ruitenberg A, Hofman A, et al. Nonsteroidal anti-inflammatory drugs and the risk of Alzheimer's disease. *N Engl J Med* 2001;345(21):1515–1521.
4. Zandi PP, Anthony JC, Hayden KM, et al. Reduced incidence of AD with NSAID but not H2 receptor antagonists: the Cache County Study. *Neurol* 2002;59(6):880–886.

Ginkgo Biloba *as a Memory Booster*

Ginkgo biloba is a plant extract containing several compounds that may have positive effects on cells within the brain through their antioxidant and anti-inflammatory properties. In addition, ginkgo may directly improve memory by enhancing the transmission of information among nerve cells. Researchers tested the ability of ginkgo to improve the memory of people who are free of Alzheimer's disease through a well-designed clinical trial. A group of 132 women and 98 men received either 40 mg of ginkgo or a sugar pill (placebo) three times a day for six weeks. While taking the pill, all volunteers underwent extensive testing of their memory, attention, learning, concentration, and other abilities. Spouses, friends, relatives, and the participants themselves also rated their memory abilities. The results were rather disappointing. After six weeks, ginkgo did not produce any measurable improvement in the volunteers' memory and other mental functions. Those who took ginkgo didn't even experience a greater subjective improvement in their memory compared with those who only took sugar pills. Based on this study, ginkgo was deemed to be ineffective as a memory enhancer in people with normal memory. Other, smaller studies contradicted this conclusion, finding that ginkgo can indeed improve memory in healthy people. Although the results are conflicting, it is safe to say that the ability of ginkgo to enhance memory (if any) in normal people is quite modest.

Ginkgo to Treat Alzheimer's Disease

While its usefulness in enhancing memory in normal people is questionable, ginkgo's other claim to fame is its purported ability to alleviate forgetfulness in people afflicted with Alzheimer's disease. This claim is not totally unfounded and may in fact be true. A reputable scientific study of people with Alzheimer's who took 120 mg of the ginkgo extract EGb761 daily for a year showed stabilization or even improvement in the mental and social decline associated with the disease compared with those who didn't take it. The extent of the improvements was not dramatic, but they were observable and measurable. Other studies are a mixed bag; some have shown ginkgo to be ineffective in treating Alzheimer's, while others have confirmed its utility for this purpose. However, when these studies are taken together, *Ginkgo biloba* is still a promising medication that has the ability to modestly improve some of the troublesome symptoms of Alzheimer's disease and other dementias.

While there is no officially recommended dose and preparation of ginkgo, most scientific studies used EGb761 at a dose of 40 mg three times a day or 80 mg twice a day. *Ginkgo biloba* is generally safe and has no serious side effects when taken in recommended amounts. Some people may experience headaches or an upset stomach. Ginkgo also has the potential of enhancing the effects of anticoagulants or blood thinners and may cause excessive bleeding. Thus, people taking anticoagulants or blood thinners such as warfarin (Coumadin), nonsteroidal anti-inflammatory

(continued)

medications like ibuprofen (Motrin, Advil) and naproxen (Aleve), or aspirin should take it only under the close supervision of their doctors. Because of the risk of bleeding, ginkgo should be stopped at least three days prior to a planned surgical procedure. Women who are pregnant or breast-feeding should also refrain from taking ginkgo because of the lack of studies that prove its safety in this group.

ANTI-INFLAMMATORY MEDICATIONS TO CURE ALZHEIMER'S DISEASE

If you were diagnosed with Alzheimer's disease today and your doctor told you that instead of an expensive prescription, you only needed to take a cheap over-the-counter medicine, you would probably be pleasantly surprised. This hope for a simple, inexpensive, and safe cure for Alzheimer's disease has triggered the launch of several clinical trials to test whether the anti-inflammatory medications naproxen (better known by its brand name Aleve) and rofecoxib (Vioxx) can be used to treat people with Alzheimer's disease. In more than thirty treatment centers around the United States, approximately 350 people with mild to moderate-stage Alzheimer's disease volunteered to participate in the study. They were divided into three groups: One received naproxen 220 mg twice a day, another took rofecoxib 25 mg once daily, and the last group took only a placebo pill. In a research technique called *double blind-*

ing, neither the researchers nor the participants knew which group they belonged to until after the end of the one-year study. The double-blinding method is commonly used in medication trials to ensure that the effect of the treatment (or lack thereof) was influenced by neither the participant's nor the researcher's prior knowledge that one medication was being taken instead of another. All participants periodically received a test of memory and other cognitive abilities to detect any improvement or worsening while on the test medication. The researchers were surprised (and probably a bit disappointed) to find that neither naproxen nor rofecoxib was able to improve the memory of people with established Alzheimer's disease. Instead of producing beneficial effects, participants who received these medications were more likely to suffer from side effects that included fatigue, dizziness, and hypertension. Critics of this study pointed out that one year may be too short a time to detect any benefit and suspect that following these people for a longer period of time may yield a different result. After all, the population-based studies only spotted the benefit of anti-inflammatory medications after two years of use. But for now, the weight of the evidence does not support the use of anti-inflammatory medications to treat people with established Alzheimer's disease. Perhaps blocking inflammation when the damage has been done—after the brain cells have died—is simply too late. The trick may be to start taking anti-inflammatory medications earlier, during the MCI phase, or even before. [Rofecoxib (Vioxx), one of the anti-inflammatory medications used in the study, was withdrawn from the market in September 2004 because it increases the risk for heart attacks.]

CAN ANTI-INFLAMMATORY MEDICINES PREVENT ALZHEIMER'S DISEASE?

Leading memory researchers believe that although ibuprofen and other anti-inflammatory medications are not effective treatments for established Alzheimer's, they may be useful in preventing susceptible people from succumbing to the disease. More skeptical scientists cautiously disagree, demanding more evidence before making any conclusions. In reality, nobody knows for sure if and how anti-inflammatory medicines can delay or prevent Alzheimer's disease. But some of the strongest proponents of this approach to Alzheimer's prevention believe that the effectiveness of ibuprofen for this purpose lies beyond its anti-inflammatory mechanism. Animal studies have shown that in addition to counteracting inflammation, medications such as ibuprofen, indomethacin, and sulindac can also decrease the production of amyloid beta, the abnormal protein that makes up the harmful amyloid plaque riddling the brains of people with Alzheimer's disease. This effect is independent of their anti-inflammatory abilities. It is scientifically plausible that these medications work by reducing inflammation and inhibiting the formation of the toxic proteins that destroy brain cells.

Scientists around the world are taking a much closer look at ibuprofen to identify which of its characteristics is truly responsible for its ability to reduce the risk for Alzheimer's. Once they discover this, the next step will be to reproduce this characteristic in a new medication that is devoid of the limiting side effects associated with high doses of ibuprofen, such as gastrointestinal bleeding and high blood pressure.

THE BOTTOM LINE ON ANTI-INFLAMMATORY MEDICINES AND ALZHEIMER'S DISEASE

Ibuprofen and other anti-inflammatory medicines have been around for more than thirty years. Only recently have they been identified as promising agents that may someday be (along with antioxidants) standard preventive measures for Alzheimer's. But more evidence is needed. The National Institutes of Health (NIH) has launched the Alzheimer's Disease Anti-inflammatory Prevention Trial (ADAPT), a clinical research study that will test the long-term safety and efficacy of the anti-inflammatory medications naproxen (Aleve) and celecoxib (Celebrex) in preventing Alzheimer's disease in people with normal memory. The results of this study are not expected to be available for years. In my clinic, I have recommended that people who have a very strong family history of Alzheimer's and have no contraindications (such as a history of gastrointestinal bleeding, kidney disease, or congestive heart failure) consider taking low doses of ibuprofen (200 mg once a day on a full stomach). This recommendation is given with the caveat that it is an unproven preventive measure and comes with a small risk of complications. Ultimately, people who are at risk of Alzheimer's must decide, in consultation with their physician, whether taking an anti-inflammatory medication is right for them. Readers are cautioned not to start taking any medicine, even over-the-counter preparations, on a regular basis without getting an okay from their doctors.

Chapter 6

The Brain–Diet Connection

"No diet will remove all the fat from your body because the brain is entirely fat. Without a brain, you might look good, but all you could do is run for public office."

—GEORGE BERNARD SHAW

You are what you eat. Innumerable diet gurus and nutritionists have espoused this short but catchy statement with the intention of motivating people to follow healthier diets. If you live for Twinkies and chocolates, you are a junk food junkie. If your definition of a Boston Marathon is ten back-to-back episodes of *Cheers* while munching on chips, you are a couch potato. And if you are a fan of low-cal diets and favor soy milk over whole milk, some people may call you a health food nut. Scientists have long suspected that diet can intimately affect not only a person's body, but his mind as well. For instance, heavy alcohol drinkers with diets devoid of essential nutrients are prone to develop Wernicke-Korsakoff syndrome, a form of brain degeneration manifesting as impairment in memory and other intellectual functions. People with this problem often make up stories to cover for their memory lapses and may also demonstrate problems with muscle coordination and vision. If the condition is not remedied by giving vitamin B_1 (thiamine) supplementation, death is certain. More recently, the composition of a person's diet has been suspected to play a role in the development of other degenerative brain diseases such as Parkinson's and Alzheimer's. Certain types of food have even been suspected of causing mood disorders like depression. These links between diet and brain disease inevitably lead to the question: Can a healthier diet truly lead to a healthier mind? In the following sections, I will discuss the connection between what and how much we eat and our risks for memory problems and Alzheimer's disease.

LOW-CALORIE DIET AND AGING

Mary Salomone was sixty-five years old but looked like she was eighty; a lack of sunlight exposure gave her skin a pale, dingy tone that made her look much older than her chronological age. Though only vague traces of it remain in her face, Mary was beautiful in her youth. She got pregnant and was forced to get married a day short of her seventeenth birthday. On her honeymoon, she suffered a miscarriage and a botched operation resulted in the loss of her fertility, sending her on a downward spiral of depression. Mary became a widow at twenty-eight and never remarried. Food became her constant companion. She passed her days crocheting, watching television, and stuffing her mouth with food that was sweet or greasy, often both. She was a regular at the buffet line of the local Chinese food restaurant and was on a first-name basis with the kids behind the counter at McDonald's.

Mary's primary care physician had tried many times to convince her to lose some weight. "Vegetables are for rabbits," she would say whenever he brought up the issue of her diet. Her knees, which were built to support a weight of 120 pounds, had started to buckle from the 240 pounds they had been forced to hold up for several decades. She walked with a limp from bad knee arthritis and relied on a cane for support.

Her primary physician referred Mary to me after it was brought to his attention that something in her memory was off. First, he noted that she was losing weight. This would have been a good thing except that Mary denied changing her diet. One day, her physician received a phone call from a social worker working for the state's elder protection services. According to her, they had performed a home safety evaluation on the recommendation of the fire department, which had been called into Mary's home twice during the past month after she set off the fire alarm. Apparently, Mary had been turning on the stove instead of the heater when she got cold and kept the refrigerator door open when it was warm. The social worker found her home in a state of disarray, with rotten food in the refrigerator and vermin running around. She suggested that Mary might have Alzheimer's, and that a memory specialist should see her.

Mary had none of the known risk factors for Alzheimer's disease. Her family history was clean, she had no history of head trauma, and she was still relatively young. But after I had a chance to examine her, there was no question in my mind that Mary had Alzheimer's disease. When I gave her the diagnosis, she immediately got up from her chair and gave me a big hug. She had no idea what I had just told her. As I tried to free myself from her tight grip, I wondered whether the many years of excessive calorie intake from junk food had eased her emotional wounds but somehow claimed her mind.

In industrialized countries such as the United States where food is relatively cheap and plentiful, people tend to eat more than what their bodies require to carry out functions.[1] Unhealthy foods are generally cheaper, more accessible, and have longer shelf lives than healthy ones such as fresh fruits and vegetables. American restaurants and fast food chains dole out huge portions of fatty foods to remain competitive in the "more is better" marketplace. Although the bad effects of a high-calorie, high-fat diet to the heart have been proclaimed repeatedly since the links among cholesterol, obesity, and heart disease were established, not many people are aware of the evidence that supports the strong connection between a high-calorie diet and the aging of other organ systems. Overeating can accelerate the body's aging process and cause the premature appearance of age-related diseases. I'm almost certain that had Mary consumed a balanced, low-calorie diet, she would have had a longer and healthier life.

THE BAD EFFECTS OF OVEREATING

One popular theory on how overeating can cause an acceleration of the aging process is through the generation of the bad forms of oxygen previously discussed as one of the possible causes of Alzheimer's disease. Whenever we eat something, a

1. Mattson MP. *Diet-Brain Connections: Impact on Memory, Mood, Aging and Disease.* Norwell, MA: Kluwer Academic Publishers, 2002.

complicated chain of chemical reactions is triggered that ultimately results in the conversion of the calories in the food we eat to energy that will either be used to fuel our daily activities or be stored as complex carbohydrates or fat for later use. Diet and exercise gurus refer to this process as "burning calories"; scientists call it the oxidation of food. The conversion of food calories to a form that can be used by our bodies involves the addition of oxygen into the mix. And as with any chemical reaction that involves oxygen, this one also produces harmful oxygen free radicals in the process. Our bodies have natural antioxidants that neutralize these toxic forms of oxygen to prevent them from causing damage to our cells. In theory, the combined amounts of antioxidants from the food we consume and the ones produced by our bodies should be enough to counter the harmful effects of oxygen radicals generated by a normal diet. But overeating is a different story; the consumption of a high-calorie diet demands more chemical reactions to convert the food to usable forms. In the process, greater amounts of harmful oxygen free radicals are generated, and they can use up our reserve of natural antioxidants. Consequently, if our diets don't provide additional antioxidants (from fruits and vegetables or supplements) to replenish our dwindling reserves, oxygen radicals are able to wreak havoc on our bodies.

Of Mice and Men: The Benefits of Calorie Restriction to Brain Health

Studies have shown that the life span of simple organisms like yeasts, and more complicated ones such as rodents and monkeys, can be increased by as much as 50 percent by simply reducing their caloric intake. In humans, a low-calorie diet can decrease the incidence of not only heart disease, but also age-related cancers and diabetes.

To look at the specific effects of calorie restriction on brain longevity, scientists experimented on rats and mice by feeding them a low-calorie diet. The rodents either received food only every other day or ate every day but consumed food pellets that contained 30 to 40 percent fewer calories than their usual food. These were then compared with rodents that consumed the usual high-calorie diet. As it turns out, the calorie-restricted mice and rats lived 30 to 40 percent longer than those that ate the usual diet. But more than just increasing their life span, the low-cal diet left the rodents' brains resistant to the effects of noxious agents that mimicked the effects of aging and degenerative diseases.[2] These experiments informed us that restricting calories is good for the rodent brain. But drastically reducing the caloric intake of humans with the hope of delaying or preventing degenerative diseases is an entirely different ball game. First of all, finding a significant number of people who would be willing to eat only every other day for several years is next to impossible. Even if we did find willing volunteers, such starvation protocols would be hazardous and ethically unacceptable. The only safe and practical way to examine the link between caloric intake and brain health is to closely observe large populations of people with different patterns of caloric intake and see if these differences seem to translate into the development of memory problems. If caloric restriction in humans can indeed protect the brain from degenerative diseases, people with

2. Bruce-Keller AJ, Umberger G, McFall R, Mattson MP. Food restriction reduces brain damage and improves behavioral outcome following excitotoxic and metabolic insults. *Ann Neurol* 1999;45:8–15.

> ## *Calories and Alzheimer's*
>
> Alzheimer's disease incidence in China and Japan is about half that seen in the United States and Western Europe. This observation suggests the possibility that the low-calorie diet followed by Eastern cultures protects their brain from degenerative diseases.

lower daily caloric intakes should have a correspondingly lower risk of Alzheimer's disease.

To solve this mystery, scientists turned to the Far East. In China and Japan, where the typical diet is rich in fruits and vegetables, the usual daily calorie intake ranges from sixteen hundred to two thousand calories. This is considerably lower in calories than the typical American and Western European diet, which is somewhere between twenty-five hundred and three thousand calories a day. Studies have shown a strong link between per capita food consumption and the risk of Alzheimer's.[3] While these striking geographic differences in dietary intake and Alzheimer's disease incidence are suggestive, they are not irrefutable evidence that calorie restriction is good for the human brain. This is because of the existence of alternate explanations for the observed differences, such as genetic or racial differences and varying methods of identifying individuals with memory problems in such large population studies.

A more reliable way to test whether calorie-restricted diets can indeed prevent Alzheimer's and other degenerative diseases is to look at racially homogeneous populations that have

3. Grant W. Dietary links to Alzheimer's disease. *Alzheimer's Disease Rev* 1997;2:42–55.

more uniform food intake. Standard methods must also be used to identify members of the population with Alzheimer's disease. One such study involved a group of individuals living in the Washington Heights area of New York City.[4] The researchers estimated each person's average caloric intake by means of a food-frequency questionnaire that included sixty-one different types of food. The 980 volunteers were asked how often they ate each type of food, the breakfast cereals they consumed, how much sugar and salt they used, and even the type of fat they used for baking and frying. Although it was virtually impossible to rigidly control the participants' caloric intake the way a laboratory mouse's could be, the volunteers' honest answers to these questions provided a good snapshot of their patterns of food consumption. As expected, in this group of aging New Yorkers, those who had the highest daily caloric intakes were also at the greatest risk of developing Alzheimer's disease. Conversely, those who reported the lowest caloric intakes appeared to be protected.

Calories and Brain Disease

Studies have shown that low-calorie diets can also effectively lower the risks for other brain diseases, such as Parkinson's disease and strokes. These findings reinforce the promising beneficial effect of caloric restriction for the overall protection of the human brain against degenerative conditions.

4. Luchsinger JA, Tang M, Shea S, Mayeux R. Caloric intake and the risk of Alzheimer's disease. *Arch Neurol* 2002;59(8):1258–1263.

Starve the Brain, Feed the Mind?

The body of evidence that supports the bad effects of overeating and the health-promoting capabilities of caloric restriction is rapidly accumulating. It is currently one of the hottest areas in aging research. Scientists hope to someday establish beyond a doubt that aging and all the nefarious things that go with it can be indefinitely postponed simply by reducing the amount of food and calories we consume. Take note that in the prevention of Alzheimer's disease, maintaining an ideal weight may not be enough. Studies have shown that the risk of Alzheimer's disease is more closely linked to caloric intake than to weight or body mass index (BMI). This means that a junk food junkie who is blessed with a high metabolic rate that keeps her from gaining weight may still be at a higher risk for developing a memory problem. If we consider the logic that explains how caloric restriction exerts its beneficial effects on the body and mind, this makes a lot of sense. The amount of age-accelerating oxygen free radicals generated from our diet is related to the amount of calories we consume, not to our weight. Thus a person with a high metabolic rate who consumes greater calories may actually be producing more harmful forms of oxygen than someone with a slower metabolic rate.

In addition to decreasing oxidative damage, caloric restriction may have other health benefits. It is thought to induce a stress response in the brain that directly stimulates it to produce more nerve cells to compensate for those lost to aging and disease. Restricting calories is likewise good for the heart, reduces the chance of getting diabetes, and protects us from the bad health effects associated with obesity. For all these reasons, caloric restriction may be the ideal way to keep Alzheimer's and other diseases at bay. At present, the average daily caloric intake of Americans is approximately twenty-seven hundred calories for women and more than three thousand for men. I advise you to consider restricting your intake to about eighteen to twenty-two hundred calories per day. Although highly active people may need slightly more, this daily caloric allowance is enough to sustain most moderately active adults.

We all know that restricting the caloric consumption of a generation whose staple diet consists of supersized portions of fatty foods is easier said than done. Scientists are hard at work to figure out the mechanism by which caloric restriction delays the aging process. Once this is revealed, the next step will be to find a way to mimic the effects of a calorie-restricted diet to derive the benefits associated with it. However, we are presently years, if not decades, away from this discovery. Until then, we must choose what we eat wisely: This may ultimately determine the fate of not only our bodies, but also our minds.

DIETARY FATS AND THE FATTY BRAIN

Fats and cholesterol normally makes up 70 percent of the human brain. Thus, in a purely biochemical sense, the brain is not much more than a mound of fat. But unlike the other fat collections of the body such as those in the gut and buttocks that are mere energy depots, brain fats are specialized to perform vital functions and are highly metabolic. This plasticity is what allows us to form a thought or hold a memory while selectively screening out numerous stimuli that our five senses receive from the environment. The hardworking human brain needs a constant supply of fats and cholesterol to maintain and repair itself. However, it must also find an efficient way to clear the excess fat, which can be very toxic to the sensitive nerve cells. Consequently, the brain is always in the process of maintaining the delicate balance between the fat that it uses and the fat that it needs to eliminate. The brain must be able to recognize and handle the different types of fats if it is to maintain this balance.

Fish Fat as Brain Food

Although the two types of fats in the food we consume have only minor differences in their molecular structure, these differences are enough for each to have profoundly distinct effects on the body. *Saturated fat* is considered the unhealthy or "bad" form of dietary fat. It is present in foods such as meat, cookies, pastries, and dairy products. When taken in large amounts over many years, saturated fats can increase the risk of a heart attack and stroke. *Unsaturated fats,* on the other hand, are considered the healthy or "good" fat. These are further subdivided into *monounsaturated fatty acid (MUFA)* and *polyunsaturated fatty acid (PUFA).* Olive oil is a common source of MUFA, while PUFA is abundant in vegetable oils. *Eicosapentaenoic acid (EPA)* and *docosahexaenoic acid (DHA)* are special types of PUFAs found in fatty cold-water fish such as albacore tuna, lake trout, salmon, and mackerel. Together, EPA and DHA are more commonly known as *omega-3 fatty acids.* These types of fat are especially good for the heart because they can reduce triglyceride levels, lower the blood pressure, and decrease the risks for heart attacks and strokes. EPA and DHA are the active ingredients of many popular fish oil supplements.

A typical diet consists of varying amounts of both the good and bad types of fat. Unsaturated types of fat have been shown to be good for the heart, while the saturated ones are outright harmful. Scientists have questioned whether the good fat–bad fat mechanism also holds true for the brain–and if so, what kinds of fat are good for the brain and which types are harmful? A large population-based study conducted in the suburb of Rotterdam, the Netherlands, shed some light into this mystery. About seven hundred residents of the town participated in this study. The Dutch scientist gave the participants a food-frequency questionnaire that included information on how much and what types of fat they typically consumed. They then followed these people over the course of two years, looking for the development of memory problems. The results were encouraging. Just like the heart, the brain appears to benefit from certain types of dietary fat and suffer from others. Specifically, a diet high in saturated fat and cholesterol increased the risk of dementia. In contrast, eating more than 20 grams of fish (a food rich in omega-3 fatty acids) a day lowered the risk of developing Alzheimer's disease.[5]

Another study that investigated this connection between regular fish consumption and the brain came from researchers

> ### *Health Benefits of Fish Intake*
>
> **In addition to helping reduce Alzheimer's risk, fish intake is believed to reduce the risks for a heart attack, stroke, and even certain forms of cancers, such as those of the prostate and gastrointestinal tract.**

5. Kalmijn S, Llauner LF, Ott A, et al. Dietary fat intake and the risk of incident dementia in the Rotterdam Study. *Ann Neurol* 1997;42:776–782.

based at Rush University, who examined a group of more than eight hundred individuals living in Chicago. They found that people who ate fish at least once a week had 60 percent less risk of developing Alzheimer's than those who consumed fish less frequently.[6] While the researchers don't know exactly how regular fish consumption lowers the risk for Alzheimer's, they believe that its rich omega-3 fatty acid content has something to do with it. Note that these studies point to a beneficial effect of the regular consumption of fish and may not necessarily translate to the intake of fish oil supplements.

High Cholesterol Levels and Alzheimer's Disease

If you are between the ages of forty and fifty-nine years and your cholesterol level is more than 251 mg/dl (6.5 mmol/L), you are at a greater risk of succumbing to Alzheimer's disease in the future. This is the finding of a Finnish study that examined the relationship between serum cholesterol levels and the risk of Alzheimer's disease.[7] Some of my patients with borderline high cholesterol have asked me whether they should reduce their cholesterol levels to prevent Alzheimer's disease. At the Framingham Heart Study, my colleagues and I challenged the cholesterol–Alzheimer's link by looking at the relationship between the average blood cholesterol levels of more than a thousand people taken over a thirty-year period and their risk of developing Alzheimer's disease more than a decade later. We found that having a high lifetime cholesterol

6. Morris MC, Evans DA, Bienias JL, et al. Consumption of fish and n-3 fatty acids and risk of incident Alzheimer's disease. *Arch Neurol* 2003;60:940–946.
7. Notkola IL, Sulkava R, Pekkanen J, et al. Serum total cholesterol, Apolipoprotein E4 allele, and Alzheimer's disease. *Neuroepidemiol* 1998;17:14–20.

level does not necessarily increase the risk of developing Alzheimer's later—and conversely, a low cholesterol level does not offer any significant protection from the disease.[8] While this finding does not invalidate the results of previous studies, it does raise the question: Is cholesterol really related to Alzheimer's disease, or is it only a marker for other lifestyle factors? For instance, people with diets rich in good fats and low in bad fats and cholesterol may also consume fewer calories, exercise more, and follow a generally healthier lifestyle. Thus, while keeping your cholesterol at a low level is good for the heart, it does not appear to help in preventing Alzheimer's disease.

Skimming the Fat

It is safe to say that the jury is still out when it comes to the possible link between fats and Alzheimer's disease. However, we do know that in the case of dietary fat intake and overall brain and body health, the verdict is definitely in. For disease prevention, the type of fat we consume is more important than the actual amount we take. A diet high in saturated fat and cholesterol can lead to the development of heart disease and even increase the risk of getting a stroke. In contrast, a diet high in unsaturated fats, especially the omega-3 fatty acids found in fish, has many good effects on the heart and may even decrease the risk for Alzheimer's disease. Before deciding to take fish oils and other supplements, you should discuss it with your doctor to make sure that this is right for you.

---

8. Tan ZS, Seshadri S, Beiser A, et al. Plasma total cholesterol level as a risk factor for Alzheimer's disease: The Framingham Study. *Arch Internal Med* 2003;163;1053–1057.

A Heart-Healthy Diet

The American Heart Association (AHA) recommends a diet low in saturated fat and the regular consumption of foods rich in unsaturated fats. For people without known heart disease, a balanced diet that includes fatty fishes such as salmon, sardines, and tuna at least once or twice a week should be sufficient. But for people with known coronary heart disease or those with high triglyceride levels, a higher amount of omega-3 fatty acids is recommended. For example, a person with an elevated triglyceride level may need to take as much as 2 to 4 grams of omega-3 fatty acids a day in the form of capsules. At high doses (greater than 3 grams per day), these supplements can cause bleeding in certain people. They can also increase the levels of bad (LDL) cholesterols, making them unsuitable for people with high cholesterol levels. These recommendations can be found at the AHA Web site, www.americanheart.org.

However, I recommend that everyone should limit their intake of saturated fats in favor of unsaturated fats in their diet.

ALCOHOL AND MEMORY

Anyone who has ever had one drink too many knows how difficult it is to walk a straight line, much less think straight. This is why the standard field sobriety test used by police officers for suspected DUI drivers includes not only tests for coordination such as standing on one leg and walking heel-to-toe on a straight line, but also mental tests such as counting backward and reciting the alphabet. While alcohol in small to moderate amounts can feel like a stimulant, higher doses can temporarily depress many of the brain's functions. In the longer term, alcohol abuse can result in permanent mental impairments by inducing nutritional deficiencies and producing traumatic head injuries.

Most people do not consider alcohol as something that can directly produce permanent memory deficits. But several studies have shown that repeated exposure to high levels of alcohol can cause tissue damage in several organs, including the brain. Excessive amounts of alcohol are directly toxic to the brain cells that hold our memories and control vital mental functions. Chronic alcohol consumption results in a significant loss of brain tissue and a higher incidence of memory problems.

There is no question that too much alcohol is bad news for the brain. However, light to moderate alcohol intake may be a different story. The health benefits of modest alcohol consumption are now well known: It can help prevent heart attacks and reduce the risk for a stroke. Unfortunately, the effects of light to moderate amounts of alcohol intake on memory are less well defined. Studies looking into this association have yielded conflicting results, with some showing a protective effect while others showing no effect at all. However, a large population-based study of more than eighteen hundred Swedish volunteers showed that light to moderate alcohol intake can lower the risk of Alzheimer's disease.[9] Another study followed more than three thousand Japanese men

9. Huang W, Qiu C, Winblad B, Fratiglioni L. Alcohol consumption and incidence of dementia in a community sample aged 75 years and older. *J Clin Epidemiol* 2002;55:959–964.

for eighteen years to see how their alcohol consumption patterns affected their memory as they aged. The researchers found that those who drank up to one alcoholic beverage per day performed better on memory tests than those who did not consume alcohol at all. However, those who had more than one drink a day achieved lower scores on the memory tests than the nondrinkers. There was a pattern of worsening performance with higher alcohol intake, with the worst memory test scores achieved by those who consumed four or more drinks a day.[10] Proponents of this relationship believe that alcohol exerts its beneficial effects on the brain in the same way it does on the heart. That is, alcohol increases the levels of good (HDL) cholesterol, keeps blood vessels healthy, and ensures adequate blood supply to the brain. The potent antioxidants found in red wine (flavonoids) are also suspected to play a role in warding off memory problems.

The studies that support the ability of alcohol to chase Alzheimer's away are far from definitive. While it is plausible that the beneficial effects of moderate alcohol consumption on the heart likewise hold true for the mind, I would not encourage nondrinkers to start taking alcohol to avoid memory problems. The lack of adequate scientific proof of benefit and the difficulty of identifying those at risk of succumbing to alcoholism make this approach too risky. Regular alcohol drinkers are strongly advised to do so in moderation. In general, men should take no more than one or two drinks per day, while women should take only one drink a day.[11]

10. Galanis DJ, Joseph C, Masaki KH, et al. A longitudinal study of drinking and cognitive performance in elderly Japanese American men: The Honolulu-Asia Aging Study. *Am J Pub Health* 2000;90:1254–1259.

11. A drink is one twelve-ounce beer, four ounces of wine, an ounce and a half of eighty-proof spirits, or one ounce of hundred-proof spirits.

Chapter 7

Learn Now, Age Later

"What we learn with pleasure we never forget."
—ALFRED MERCIER

Every day, your five senses are bombarded with a multitude of new stimuli that need to be processed and screened by your brain. To avoid information overload, your mind consciously or unconsciously holds on to information that it considers important and discards the rest. At the microscopic level, this occurs when a brain cell extends one of its many arms to form a new connection with another nerve cell. The connections or *synapses* between the brain cells allow for more efficient communication, helping with the transfer, storage, and retrieval of information. Thus, on any given day, the number of new connections formed within your brain is truly huge. The *synaptic density* of a brain is a measure of the abundance of these connections. The higher your synaptic density, the more connections there are among your brain cells, giving the mind greater efficiency and resistance against memory disorders. This is the characteristic I referred to in chapter 2 as *brain plasticity*. Since a new connection between brain cells is formed whenever we learn something new, it only makes sense that smart and highly educated people are less likely to succumb to memory problems. This is what researchers sought to prove by looking closely at the mind of a group of aging nuns. In this chapter, I'll describe the fascinating Nun Study and tell you the most important discoveries from this and similar studies that examined the connection between lifelong learning and aging of the mind.

THE SECRET OF THE NUNS

In 1986, a priceless treasure was discovered at the convent of the Sisters of Notre Dame in Mankato, Minnesota. The treasure was not in the form of precious stones, gold bars, or even rare art. They were volumes of notes held by dusty green binders in old file drawers that weren't worth very much until Dr. David Snowdon, a researcher on aging at the University of Minnesota, stumbled upon them. Buried in those pages were the autobiographies of the nuns written almost sixty years earlier as part of their entry into religious life. Before they took their religious vows, the then twenty-two-year-old nuns purged themselves of the secular world by pouring out the contents of their hearts and minds in words, phrases, and sentences. Each described the path that led her to the convent and the hopes and dreams she carried with her along the way. The discoveries were so significant that other Notre Dame nuns who lived throughout the Midwestern, Eastern, and Southern regions of the United States were invited to participate. At present, the Nun Study, as it is now popularly called, has 678 of these women who submit faithfully to comprehensive examinations meant to show their differential patterns of aging and susceptibility to mental decline. The participants ranged in age from 75 to 102 years at the beginning of the study in 1991. At the time of this writing, the oldest member has survived to 107 years of age.

The revelations of the Nun Study have shed light into some of the darkest mysteries of the aging mind. For instance, the researchers found that certain traits of early adulthood could be used to predict the nuns' risk of developing Alzheimer's disease many decades later. Specifically, they identified that linguistic ability, as measured by the idea density and grammatical complexity of the early autobiographies, is a good way to identify those at a higher risk of mental decline. The women who had the lowest idea density and grammatical complexity in early adulthood also had the highest chance for poor intellectual performance and Alzheimer's disease in their later years.[1] This finding suggests that a good linguistic ability during early adulthood can somehow protect the brain from degenerative disorders such as Alzheimer's disease. Since linguistic ability is known to be closely related to education, the researchers also examined the possible link between the number of years of formal schooling and the risk of memory problems. Similar to the finding for linguistic ability, the nuns who held college degrees were far more likely to maintain their intellectual capacity well into old age than were their counterparts who had fewer years of education. These highly educated nuns were also observed to lead longer and

1. Snowdon DA, Kemper SJ, Mortimer JA, et al. Linguistic ability in early life and cognitive function and Alzheimer's disease in late life: findings from the Nun Study. *J Am Med Assoc* 1996;275:528–532.

more independent lives, an average of over three good functioning years longer even after the age of seventy-five.[2]

The significance of these discoveries goes well beyond the intriguing results. As poignantly put by one participant, the Nun Study allows the Sisters of Notre Dame to keep teaching all of us about aging and the brain even after their death. The same selfless dedication that compelled these women to participate in the study has prompted them to also donate their brain to science after their death. The brain donation program of the Nun Study has allowed researchers to examine the brains of several of the oldest nuns. They found that the brains of some of the women who remained free of Alzheimer's until the time of their death had the characteristic plaques and tangles that are typically seen only in those suffering from the disease. In other words, several nuns who, based on the appearance of their brain alone, should have developed Alzheimer's before they died—didn't. Instead, they remained intellectually intact until the very end. The only way to explain this phenomenon is the existence of other factors or characteristics that kept the nuns' brains resistant to Alzheimer's disease. The Nun Study researchers believe that several important factors account for this, including the amount of brain tissue and synapses developed in early life, the amount and severity of brain damage from head trauma and strokes in middle and late life, and the lifelong nutritional status that makes the brain more or less vulnerable to damage.[3] Additionally, the researchers believe that mental training even during later years could affect the brain's ability to remain intact.

2. Snowdon DA, Ostwald SK, Kane RL, Keenan NL. Years of life with good and poor mental and physical function in the elderly. *J Clin Epidemiol* 1989;42:1055–1066.
3. Snowden, David A. Healthy aging and dementia: from the Nun Study. *Ann Internal Med* 2003;139:450–454.

The nuns' baseline linguistic abilities and level of education were likely to be just surrogate measures of their brains' underlying synaptic density and plasticity. The higher number of cells and connections among these cells in the brains of the most intelligent and well-educated nuns likely played a role in the preservation of their minds.

The fact that the brains of very smart people are not identical to those of regular folks has been shown elsewhere. The nuns are not the only people whose brains continue to educate us about the secrets of the smart mind and the aging brain. The passing of one of the greatest teachers of our generation has provided us valuable information on the links that connect intelligence, learning, and the brain's physical structure.

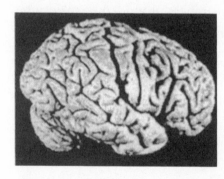

A 1955 photograph of Albert Einstein's brain.

Reprinted with permission from Witelson SF, Elsevier. *Lancet* 1999; 253:2150.

ALBERT EINSTEIN'S BRAIN

The great mathematician and scientist Albert Einstein died at 1:15 A.M. on April 18, 1955. He was seventy-six years old. Before his death, he requested that his body be cremated but that his brain be saved and studied for research. Dr. Thomas Harvey, who was then the chief pathologist at Princeton

Hospital in New Jersey, went to work later that day to carefully extract the precious brain of the genius.[4] Thereafter, the exact location and condition of Einstein's brain were mysteries for more than twenty years. But in 1978, journalist Steven Levy, now senior editor at *Newsweek,* tracked down the organ and broke the news in an article published in the August 1978 issue of *New Jersey Monthly.* He discovered that Dr. Harvey had since moved to Wichita, Kansas, and had taken Einstein's brain with him. He kept it in his study, safely tucked away inside two mason jars filled with formaldehyde. The jars were hidden inside an unassuming cardboard box labeled COSTA CIDER.[5] But by the time it was rediscovered, the brain of the genius was no longer in one piece. Over the years, Dr. Harvey had cut the brain up into about 240 pieces and distributed some of them to leading researchers around the world who were seeking to unravel the mystery behind Einstein's genius.

Dr. Manan Diamond of the University of California at Berkeley led one such group of fortunate scientists who had the opportunity to study Einstein's brain. They decided that the best way to go about this task was to compare his brain with those of eleven other males of average intelligence. The researchers analyzed a piece of Einstein's brain under the microscope and counted the number of nerve cells and glial cells in the different areas of each brain. Glial cells, as you may recall from the first chapter, play a supporting role to the brain's nerve cells by providing nutrition and repairing damage. Dr. Diamond and her group found that compared with the "normal" brains, Einstein's brain demonstrated a disproportionately higher

4. Abraham C. *Possessing Genius: The Bizarre Odyssey of Einstein's Brain.* New York: St. Martin's Press, 2002.
5. Levy S. I found Einstein's brain. http://www.stevenlevy.com/einstein.html.

number of glial cells in the region of the brain called Area 39. This area, located in the left parietal brain cortex, is known to be involved in language and other complex functions. The authors concluded that the increased number of supporting glial cells in this particular part of Einstein's brain was likely a compensatory reaction to the increased metabolic requirements needed to support his unusually robust intellectual activity.[6]

Researchers from the University of Alabama at Birmingham also had a chance to examine Einstein's brain. They found that his brain weighed a relatively measly 1,230 grams. This is significantly lighter than the weight of an average male brain of approximately fourteen hundred grams. When they looked at it more closely, however, they were surprised to discover that the relatively light and thin brain was populated with a much higher density of brain cells than the average brain.[7] This means that for a given area of cerebral cortex, his brain packed more brain cells—probably accounting for his unusual intellectual abilities.

The latest findings on Einstein's brain come from Dr. Sandra Witelson and her colleagues at McMaster University in Ontario, Canada. Like earlier studies, they confirmed that the brain of the genius is not identical to the brains of people with average intelligence. Specifically, the Canadian researchers found that the inferior parietal lobe—an area of the brain associated with mathematical abilities, music, and processing of visual images—was 15 percent wider in Einstein's brain than other brains. Interestingly, they also found that a groove that

6. Diamond MC, Scheibel AB, Murphy GM, Harvey T. On the brain of a scientist: Albert Einstein. *Exper Neurol* 1985;88(1):198–204.

7. Anderson B, Harvey T. Alteration in cortical thickness and neuronal density in the frontal cortex of Albert Einstein. *Neurosci Lett* 1996;210:161–164.

normally separates parts of the brain from each other was partially missing.[8] They believe that this unique brain configuration allowed Einstein's abundant brain cells to make connections more easily with each other and function more efficiently.

EDUCATION AND ALZHEIMER'S DISEASE

Most will agree that a genius like Einstein is born and not made. Yet it is highly unlikely for a genius to attain the mind's full potential if he does not exert the effort to learn his craft. Education fosters lifelong learning and frequently leads people to challenging occupations. Studies have shown that people who have high levels of education or whose occupations constantly require a high degree of complex mental functions are at a lower risk of developing Alzheimer's disease. Several theories have been offered to explain this inverse relationship between the level of education and the incidence of Alzheimer's disease. These range from the simple contention that highly educated or intelligent people are just better test takers, to the belief that a higher functional brain reserve (owing to a greater density of brain synaptic connections) offers protection to the brain against Alzheimer's.[9] Whatever the explanation, we cannot overlook the fact that highly educated people and those with mentally challenging occupations stand a better chance of keeping their minds in-

8. Witelson SF, Kigar DL, Harvey T. The exceptional brain of Albert Einstein. *Lancet* 1999;353:2149–2153.
9. Katzman R. Education and the prevalence of dementia and Alzheimer's disease. *Neurol* 1993;43:13–20.

tact well into old age. Because we cannot turn back the hands of time to change the circumstances of our birth and youth that led us to where we are now intellectually, the more important question becomes: Are there things we can do now to alter the fate of our minds in the future?

The Brain Exercise Experiment

The accruing evidence that education and challenging occupations can help maintain a person's intellectual abilities led Dr. George Rebok of the Johns Hopkins University and his colleagues to examine whether mental training in later life can really prevent age-related declines in intellectual functions. Nearly three thousand volunteers residing in six U.S. metropolitan areas participated in what was known as the ACTIVE trial. This study tested the effectiveness of brain exercises to improve a person's memory, intellectual abilities, and daily functioning. The participants ranged in age from sixty-five to ninety-four years and had no evidence of MCI or Alzheimer's disease. They were randomly assigned to one of four groups and received training in one of three specific mental abilities: memory (ability to remember), reasoning (ability to solve problems that follow a serial pattern), and speed of mental processing. The fourth group received training in none of these and served as a comparison for the other three groups.

People who received memory training were taught strategies for remembering word lists and sequences and how to pick out the details and main ideas of

(continued)

stories. Reasoning training involved the use of techniques to solve problems that follow a serial pattern, such as prescription drug schedules or a travel itinerary. Participants who received training in speed of processing learned to hone their visual search skills and their ability to quickly locate visual information while being distracted by another stimulus. Each person was tested periodically over the two-year study period, and each performance was compared to the participant's own baseline abilities and to the members of the group who did not receive any training.

After only ten mental exercise sessions, Dr. Rebok and his colleagues noted significant improvements in the volunteers' abilities to perform mental tasks related to the training they received. In fact, the magnitude of improvement was equivalent to the decline in the same abilities that can be expected to occur over a seven- to fourteen-year period. The improvements were also durable, persisting until the study was concluded two years later. Whether the improvement in mental performance gained from the brain exercises can last longer than two years and whether it can improve a person's daily function is the subject of ongoing investigation. But the results of this study suggest that keeping our minds active during our later years can indeed prevent or even *reverse* the decline in mental abilities that are observed as part of "normal" aging. In the Memory Improvement Program found in chapter 12, Dr. George Rebok and I collaborate to provide you with some memory improvement techniques and exercises similar to those used in the ACTIVE trial to work your mind into the best shape possible.

LEISURE ACTIVITIES AND ALZHEIMER'S DISEASE

Most of us who toil hard every day to make a living can hardly wait to reach the age of retirement. Our reasons for looking forward to the age of sixty-five are almost as varied as the types of work we perform. Some of us are planning long trips to visit family and friends, others to explore far and exotic places; many will work on their gardens or learn a new hobby. But most of us are simply looking forward to kicking back and relaxing in our backyards on a warm summer day, reading a good book while sipping on a tall glass of ice-cold lemonade. How you choose to spend your later years is entirely up to you. But if you intend to keep your mind as sharp as possible after the age of retirement, you should keep the "use it or lose it" adage in mind. Most of us have observed or at least heard of older people whose memory and intellectual abilities decline precipitously soon after they stop working and retreat to a physically and mentally sedentary lifestyle, while others thrive in mind and body after they are freed from the restraints of a nine-to-five job and are finally able to immerse themselves in the leisure activities they truly love. In the next few pages, we'll explore the best ways to spend our leisure time and how keeping mentally active during our later years can affect the viability of our minds.

An Aging Bronx Tale

The Bronx borough of New York City is one of the most ethnically diverse neighborhoods in the United States. It is also the setting for one of the most prominent studies that examined

The Additive Effect of Mental Exercise

In practical terms, someone who does the *New York Times* crossword puzzles four days a week has an almost 50 percent lower risk of developing Alzheimer's than her next-door neighbor who only does the puzzle once a week!

whether participation in leisure activities can effectively ward off intellectual decline in older people. The Bronx Aging Study analyzed the lifestyle of 469 elderly people living in the Bronx and rated their level of participation in leisure activities. Specifically, the volunteers were asked whether they regularly engaged in mental activities such as reading books and newspapers, writing for pleasure, doing crossword puzzles, playing board or card games, playing musical instruments, and participating in organized group discussions. Each person received a score according to the degree and frequency of participation in these activities. The participants were then observed in order to watch the development of memory and intellectual decline over the next twenty-one years.[10]

This study found that while participating regularly in leisure activities is beneficial, not all types of mental and physical activities are equally effective in preventing memory and intellectual decline. The mental leisure activities that were particularly effective in protecting the brain against the development of Alzheimer's disease are:

1. Reading
2. Playing board games
3. Playing musical instruments

10. Verghese J, Lipton RB, Katz M, et al. Leisure activities and the risk of dementia in the elderly. *N Engl J Med* 2003;348:2508–2516.

The researchers also discovered that when it came to mental activities and brain protection, more is definitely better. That is, the more often a person engaged in leisure activities, the lower their risk of dementia. In fact, people who participated in the activities frequently (three or four times a week) were more than 60 percent less likely to succumb to memory problems than were those who participated in these activities least frequently. In the next chapter, I will discuss in greater detail some of the leisure activities that are most effective in preserving brain health.

USE IT OR LOSE IT?

During the deepest stages of sleep, our muscles relax and our body's metabolism slows down dramatically. Even our temperature drops, and our breathing becomes shallow. Surprisingly, it is at this time, when the rest of the body is essentially in a state of near shutdown, that the mind is most active. In fact, the brain needs to paralyze our voluntary muscles to prevent us from acting out our vivid dreams and hurting ourselves in the process. Brain wave activity measurements taken during deep sleep are similar in pattern to those taken while a person is wide awake and thinking. This proves that our minds are working overtime even while we are deep in slumber.

What your mind does while you are asleep is largely beyond your control. However, what you do with it while you are awake could spell the difference between keeping it healthy and losing it altogether. Based on the discoveries of the ACTIVE trial and other studies of the aging mind, it is fair to say that intellectual stimulation during later years is beneficial to the mind and *can help ward off or even reverse the age-related decline in memory*. Nobody knows the specific types and the exact amounts of intellectual activity necessary to accomplish this. But according to available evidence, it's not likely to require an extraordinary amount of effort. The most important first step is to find an activity that can both stimulate your mind and spark your interest. The latter is especially important, because you are much more likely to sustain an activity that you truly enjoy. Whether it be dancing, playing a musical instrument, reading, or following a more structured memory workout program such as that found in this book, using your mind regularly is essential in keeping it intact and sharp.

Finally, I would like to emphasize that it is never too early to start a mental activity program. Many people who are still working find themselves performing repetitive and predictable work that neither challenges nor stimulates their minds. Even people with occupations that are generally considered challenging may find that after doing the same thing for many years, their work has become a ritualistic routine that they can do even in their sleep. Every one of us stands to benefit from challenging our mind and keeping it active now in preparation for our later years. A person with a healthy mind can quickly learn a new skill, expand her vocabulary, learn a new sport, or take up a new hobby. But the time may come when she will no longer be able to learn these new skills as swiftly or efficiently as she can now. For instance, while a person with a memory problem can still swing a golf club, he will be incapable of learning how to play golf if he has never done so before. The same is true for dancing, gardening, drawing, and many other activities that you can enjoy well into your old age only if you start learning to be proficient at them now. To keep your mind young tomorrow, you must start keeping yourself intellectually active today.

Chapter 8

Physical Fitness and Brain Health

"Intellectual tasting of life will not supersede muscular activity."

—Ralph Waldo Emerson

Literally translated, the popular phrase *mens sana in corpore sano* means "a sound mind in a sound body." Although this was coined by the Roman poet Juvenal nearly two thousand years ago, the latest medical research is proving the ancient statement to be true. The many health benefits of regular physical activity are well known. Exercise reduces weight, improves physical appearance, and provides a heightened sense of well-being. More important, it also has the potential to prevent many age-related diseases such as heart disease, stroke, diabetes, and osteoporosis. While the idea that a healthy mind goes hand in hand with a healthy body makes good logical sense, the ability of regular physical activity to protect the brain from Alzheimer's disease and other memory problems is a novel concept that has only recently attracted public attention.

The scientific curiosity surrounding the mysterious link between brain health and physical activity came about from the astute observation of scientists that Alzheimer's disease often coexists with diseases commonly seen in people with low levels of physical activity. Stroke and coronary heart disease, for instance, occur more commonly in people with memory problems. Since research has proven that regular physical exercise effectively reduces the risks for these diseases, it is natural to question whether Alzheimer's disease is the final result of a sedentary lifestyle. An even more important question is whether regular exercise can prevent memory problems and degenerative brain diseases.

PHYSICAL ACTIVITY AND MENTAL FITNESS

Long before its name was immortalized in a 1970s disco song, the Young Men's Christian Association (YMCA) touted the health benefits of health and fitness all over the world. In 1891, Dr. Luther Glick, a staff member at the Springfield, Massachusetts, Y and "father of physical education," proposed the now familiar Red Triangle logo of the YMCA as a symbol of a person's "essential unity—body, mind and spirit—each being a necessary and eternal part of man."

It took scientists more than a century to warm up to the possibility that the health of the mind and body are truly inseparable. They decided to test whether regular physical activity can really provide long-term mental benefits by comparing the memory and mental abilities of physically fit people with those of sedentary individuals. In the wine country of

Sonoma, California, researchers examined a group of 345 volunteers aged fifty-five years and older.[1] The participants' levels of physical fitness were assessed by measuring their peak oxygen consumption during exercise, the length of time they were able to stay on a treadmill, and the efficiency by which their bodies took up oxygen. Each person was then given the Mini Mental State Examination (MMSE), a test that offers a snapshot of memory as well as other cognitive abilities. Six years later, each participant took the MMSE again to see if any decline in mental abilities had been experienced. Lo and behold, in this group of Northern Californians, those who had the worst measures of physical fitness were found to have suffered the greatest declines in memory and other mental abilities. Based on this finding, the researchers concluded that physical fitness is indeed positively associated with mental fitness and may be useful for the preservation of memory and other intellectual functions.

THE CANADIAN AND JAPANESE EXPERIENCES

Not to be outdone by their American counterparts, Canadian researchers also examined the possible association between physical activity and memory. The Canadian Study of Health and Aging (CSHA) is a large, population-based study of about nine thousand elderly people residing in thirty-six urban and surrounding rural areas of the ten Canadian

1. Barnes DE, Yaffe K, Satariano WA, Tager B. A longitudinal study of cardiorespiratory fitness and cognitive function in healthy older adults. *J Am Ger Soc* 2003;51:459–465.

provinces. The researchers asked the participants to give details of the type, frequency, and intensity of exercise they participated in. They then followed the group for five years to see which members developed memory problems. Similar to the American study, the CSHA confirmed that when compared with people who did not exercise regularly, those who engaged in regular physical activity were less likely to succumb to Alzheimer's disease and other memory problems. Moreover, it found that the higher the level of physical activity, the lower the corresponding risk of developing Alzheimer's.[2]

In Japan, researchers followed more than eight hundred residents of the Hisayama town of Kyushu for seven years to identify the factors and characteristics that predisposed a person to Alzheimer's disease or offered protection.[3] As expected, regular physical activity figured prominently as a protective factor against memory problems. Similar to the results of the American and Canadian studies, regular physical exercise decreased the participants' risks of developing dementia. Going a step farther, yet another Japanese study tested the effectiveness of regular physical activity in improving the mental abilities of people who had established dementia. As it turns out, even regular walking can lead to improvements in the mental abilities of people with memory problems by improving their general health and providing them with a heightened sense of well-being. This suggests that regular physical activity not only helps to maintain a normal memory but can also alleviate the forgetfulness seen in

2. Laurin D, Merreault R, Lindsay J, et al. Physical activity and risk of cognitive impairment and dementia in elderly persons. *Arch Neurol* 2001;58:498–504.
3. Yoshitake T, Kiyohara Y, Kato I, et al. Incidence and risk factors of vascular dementia and Alzheimer's disease in a defined elderly Japanese population: the Hisayama Study. *Neurol* 1995;45:1161–1168.

people afflicted with Alzheimer's disease.[4] Although exercise is unlikely to cure Alzheimer's disease, it is proving to be a very useful adjunctive treatment.

DANCING ALZHEIMER'S AWAY

The discovery of an association between physical fitness and memory was certainly encouraging. Still lacking, however, were specific recommendations as to which types of physical activities are most beneficial to the brain. This question prompted the same researchers who examined the relationship between participation in mental leisure activities and memory discussed in the previous chapter to expand the scope of their investigation and ask whether certain types of physical leisure activities were more effective than others in reducing the risk of developing dementia. They asked participants whether they regularly engaged in physical activities such as playing tennis or golf, dancing, swimming, bicycling, walking for exercise, performing household chores, babysitting, and participating in team sports. Next, they asked the participants to estimate how often they engaged in each activity. The researchers then followed the memory and intellectual abilities of each person for any signs of decline.

The results of this study were pleasantly surprising. Of all the different types of physical activities, dancing was the only one that conferred beneficial effects on the mind. Contrary to the current thinking at the time that the more physically

4. Satoh T, Sakurai I, Miyagi K, Hohshaku Y. Walking exercise and improved neuropsychological functioning in elderly patients with cardiac disease. *J Internal Med* 1995;238:423–428.

demanding an activity, the more effective it is in warding off memory problems, the study showed that highly strenuous activities such as swimming and bicycling were not as effective as dancing in keeping the mind fit.

What makes dancing different? Nobody knows for sure, but one thing that distinguishes dancing from other physical activities is its unique demand for mental effort in conjunction with physical exertion. The graceful dancer listens to the music and coordinates her movements with those of her partner at the same time that she is trying to remember the complicated dance steps. She must also maintain a certain degree of mental flexibility, ready to modify the routine in the event of an unexpected misstep. It is plausible that activities that are both mentally and physically demanding can protect the brain against Alzheimer's disease when purely physical forms of leisure activities may not.

WARDING OFF ALZHEIMER'S WITH EXERCISE

Exercise is now a standard way of delaying or even completely preventing many of the diseases that plague humanity in the late stages of life. By decreasing the risks for stroke and depression, exercise has also been proven beneficial to the general health of the brain. While accumulating evidence is forging the link between exercise and memory, further study is needed to establish the connection between regular exercise and Alzheimer's disease.

The exact mechanism by which exercise protects the mind is yet to be discovered. For people with normal memory, regular exercise may alter the hormonal and physical structure of the brain itself, making it more resistant to Alzheimer's and other degenerative brain diseases. And while dancing has been shown to be effective in warding off memory problems, we still have to discover other forms of exercise that will give us the biggest bang for our buck. Many brain scientists believe that physical activities that demand both physical and mental effort stand the best chance of benefiting both mind and body. Other experts think that any type of physical exercise will confer protection to the brain against Alzheimer's by increasing its plasticity and resistance to harmful agents.[5] But whatever form of physical or mental exercise you choose to participate in, consistency is the key. Physical and mental leisure activities that are both enjoyable and sustainable are most likely to become a part of your life. So ask your physician which type of physical activity is right for you and get moving!

5. Cotman CW, Berchtold NC. Exercise: a behavioral intervention to enhance brain health and plasticity. *Trends Neurosci* 2002;25:295–301.

Chapter 9

The Mind and Body
on Estrogen

"Men never remember, but women never forget."

—UNKNOWN

Wilhelmina, Mary, Frances, Barbara. These are the names I typically see posted by the doors that line the long and sterile hallways of the senior rehabilitation hospital where I work. If you've ever had the chance to visit an assisted living or long-term care facility, you've probably noticed that most of the people who live there are women. It is common knowledge that women live longer than men. Generally speaking, women succumb to serious illnesses such as heart disease and stroke at a later age than their husbands. As a result, it has become customary for a wife to take care of her physically frail spouse in their home for several years until he takes his last breath. Unfortunately, when women get sick themselves and need someone to take care of them, their husbands are often long since gone. In industrialized countries such as the United States, most people are too busy making a living and raising their own children to be able to take care of their mothers. Thus, the cultural phenomenon that is the nursing home has thrived on the gender gap in longevity, the ever-increasing life expectancy, and the increasing burden of chronic disease.

While some women live in nursing homes because a physical disability has left them dependent on others, a significant number of them are there because a memory problem has made it unsafe for them to live alone. Studies have shown that Alzheimer's disease is more common in women than in men. Scientists first thought that this could be explained by the fact that women lived longer than their male counterparts. But even when life expectancy was taken into account, women were still found to be more likely to develop a memory problem during their lifetime than were men.

ESTROGEN AND WOMEN'S HEALTH: THE WOMEN'S HEALTH INITIATIVE

At the center of the gender gap in Alzheimer's disease risk is the hormone estrogen. This hormone has long been associated with feminine traits. But it may come as a surprise to some people that men also have a good amount of estrogen surging through their veins. Estrogen in men is produced in small quantities throughout life, giving them a low but constant exposure to the feminine hormone. In contrast, women's estrogen levels are much higher but tend to fluctuate dramatically, from an abundance in puberty to a lack in menopause.

On average, women experience ovarian failure or *menopause* sometime between the ages of forty-five and fifty-five years. Menopause is the point in a woman's life when her ovaries start to regress and degenerate. Estrogen that has bathed her vital organs for decades is abruptly withdrawn from her body. With the plummeting of her estrogen levels comes a corresponding increase in a woman's risk for many diseases; coronary heart disease, cancer, stroke, and Alzheimer's disease all become a lot more common after the onset of menopause. Doctors and scientists long suspected that this pattern was more than just coincidental. They thought that perhaps the high levels of estrogen during the reproductive period conferred protection to the body's cells and tissues against disease, and that its sharp decline after menopause explained the dramatic surge in the incidence of these serious age-related illnesses.

After menopause, women survive with very low levels of estrogen. This state of estrogen deficiency causes some to experience bothersome symptoms such as hot flashes and vaginal dryness and compels them to take estrogen replacement therapy (ERT). For many years, ERT was the standard way of treating menopausal symptoms. But many physicians believed that apart from relieving these symptoms, ERT might actually provide other health benefits to women. They argued that restoring the circulating estrogen in postmenopausal women to the levels of their youth could help avoid many age-related diseases. Consequently, in the last couple of decades, doctors shifted their prescribing patterns from short-term estrogen replacement pills for the treatment of menopausal symptoms to long-term estrogen replacement therapy with the hope of preventing disease. Researchers saw this as an opportunity to examine the health effects of long-term ERT on women's general health status and their vulnerability to different diseases. The prospect of ERT as a preventive measure for heart disease as well as other serious illnesses was so enticing that larger and more comprehensive trials were launched under the auspices of the U.S. government's National Institutes of Health.

One of the largest of these federally funded clinical trials that sought to solve the estrogen puzzle was the Women's Health Initiative (WHI). This was a set of large and well-designed clinical trials that tested the safety and efficacy of long-term estrogen replacement therapy for the prevention or treatment of diseases thought to be by-products of an estrogen-deficient state. Healthy postmenopausal women living throughout the fifty United States, with ages ranging from fifty to seventy-nine years, came in droves to volunteer for this landmark study. Because unopposed estrogen replacement therapy is known to be dangerous to women with an intact uterus, they were given a combination of estrogen and progesterone pills to mimic the natural fluctuations of these hormones during the reproductive years. Progesterone was necessary to balance the tendency of estrogen replacement therapy to cause excessive thickening of the uterine lining and endometrial cancer, a type of malignancy of the lining of the uterus. However, not all of the participants still had their uterus; some had had it surgically removed (a procedure called hysterectomy) years before for various medical reasons. These women were no longer at risk of developing endometrial cancer and therefore received only estrogen pills without the progesterone. Unbeknownst to the women, some of them only received placebo or sugar pills that were identical in appearance and taste to the estrogen and progesterone pills. This placebo group was necessary to compare both the good and the bad effects experienced by the women on hormone replacement with those who only believed they were taking it. This procedure virtually eliminated the possibility that any improvement was caused by the psychological effect of taking a pill.

THE BAD NEWS ON ESTROGEN REPLACEMENT THERAPY

The scientific world as well as the general public anxiously awaited the results of the WHI trial. It seemed intuitive that the replacement of the missing hormone would be the solution to the multitude of health problems that appeared after menopause. Some even secretly hoped for other unexpected health benefits. Perhaps, they thought, estrogen was *the* fountain of female youth that could delay aging altogether.

If there is one general lesson to be learned from the rise and fall in popularity of estrogen replacement therapy, it is that some treatments are not as useful (and safe) as they initially appear to be. This is something that the WHI researchers learned firsthand. When they decided to perform preliminary analyses of the frequency of heart disease in the women who took the estrogen and progesterone pills compared with those taking only the sugar pill, they realized that women on hormone replacement for five years had an almost 25 percent higher frequency of heart disease, especially heart attacks.[1] This finding led them to look at the frequency of other diseases, and they found that the women on ERT had more than twice the risk of developing a clot in their veins and lungs. The last straw fell when it was learned that on top of these serious problems, ERT also increased the risks for other diseases, such as breast cancer and stroke.[2] The estrogen/

---

1. Manson JE, Hsia J, Johnson KC, et al. Estrogen plus progestin and the risk of coronary heart disease. *N Engl J Med* 2003;349:523–534.
2. Risks and benefits of estrogen plus progestin in healthy postmenopausal women: principal results from Women's Health Initiative randomized controlled trial. *J Am Med Assoc* 2002; 288:321–333.

progesterone trial for the primary prevention of disease was deemed a failure and promptly discontinued three years earlier than scheduled. When the results of the WHI study were published, public health officials gave a stern warning to those who were still taking ERT to consider other alternatives. Physicians and patients heeded this warning, and millions of women dumped their estrogen pills in the garbage.

Fortunately, not all the news on estrogen replacement therapy is bad. The researchers did find that the women who took estrogen and progesterone pills enjoyed a lower risk of colorectal cancers and bone fractures. However, the investigators ultimately concluded that the risks of combined estrogen and progesterone therapy outweighed any and all of its potential benefits. Thus, based on the results of the WHI study, the use of this approach for the prevention of any disease has become medically unadvisable.

More information about estrogen replacement therapy and the Women's Health Initiative can be found on the web at: http://www.nhlbi.nih.gov/whi.

ESTROGEN AND MEMORY

The saving grace for estrogen replacement therapy may lie in its possible beneficial effects on memory. The possibility that taking estrogen after the onset of menopause can prevent Alzheimer's disease and improve memory has prompted significant interest from scientists and the general public. Alzheimer's disease and other forms of memory problems become more frequent as a woman spends more years in menopause. This fact made it tempting to jump to the conclusion that replacing estrogen could make the brain more resistant to this disease. Might there be a real link between estrogen and memory, or—as we have seen with studies of estrogen and heart disease—could this be another case of a false assumption?

From a scientific standpoint, there is substantial evidence to support estrogen's importance for normal memory and overall brain function. The human brain is sensitive to the effects of estrogen. Receptors for this hormone are found in almost every area of the brain but are particularly abundant at its base, where the cells that produce the chemical neurotransmitter called *acetylcholine* are located. This chemical is needed for the brain cells to communicate with each other. Acetylcholine levels become abnormally low in Alzheimer's disease, and certain medications treat the memory problems by increasing its concentration in the brain. The presence of estrogen receptors at the base of the brain suggests that this hormone may be able to stimulate acetylcholine's production, thereby improving function in the rest of the brain. Estrogen is also thought to directly enhance the communication lines among brain cells and even act as an antioxidant to protect the brain from damage by oxygen free radicals.

ERT and Memory

Population-based studies that examined the effect of estrogen replacement therapy on memory and other mental functions have yielded conflicting results. One study examined the memory and other mental abilities of more than eight hundred Japanese American women over the age of sixty-five who were either taking estrogen alone, estrogen combined with progesterone, or none of these. After two years, they found that the women who were taking only estrogen performed better in standardized memory tests than those who didn't take hormone replacement. However, those women who took combined estrogen and progesterone pills did not show any improvement in memory. Instead, they demonstrated a worse performance on the tests than those who did not take anything. Interestingly, the Women's Health Initiative Memory Study (WHIMS) also showed that women who took combined estrogen and progesterone pills for four years had an increased risk of developing Alzheimer's disease and other forms of dementia. [Rice MM, Groves AB, McCurry SM, et al. Postmenopausal estrogen and estrogen-progestin use and two-year cognitive change in a cohort of older Japanese American women: the Kame study. *Arch Ind Med* 2000;160:1641–1649.]

OSTEOPOROSIS AND ALZHEIMER'S: THE BONE–BRAIN LINK

No one knows for sure whether there is a critical point in time after menopause when estrogen replacement needs to be started in order to derive benefit for Alzheimer's disease prevention. But starting estrogen replacement more than a decade after menopause certainly does not appear to be beneficial, and may even be harmful to the brain and other vital organs. More recent scientific evidence suggests that postmenopausal

Estrogen and Osteoporosis

Before the Women's Health Initiative demonstrated the bad health effects of estrogen replacement therapy, estrogen was an accepted form of treatment for postmenopausal osteoporosis. Now there are safer and more effective treatments for osteoporosis. When taken along with calcium and vitamin D supplements, these can build bone and prevent future fractures.

estrogen exposure may not even be the real issue. Instead, the estrogen concentrations that a woman's brain is exposed to during her lifetime may provide a more direct link between estrogen and the brain. The amount of estrogen circulating in a woman's blood varies depending on the time of the month or even the time of day when it is measured. Thus, obtaining a single measure of circulating estrogen concentration will not give an accurate estimate of the brain's average estrogen exposure over several decades.

Bone, however, is a reliable surrogate marker to estimate the body's lifelong estrogen exposure. Although it is easy to think of bone as a lifeless collection of hard calcium that holds up and gives shape to the body, in reality it is a dynamic and living system that constantly rebuilds and reshapes itself throughout our lifetime. If you fell and broke your arm, for instance, the doctor would need to put it in a cast that holds it in place for the several weeks or months required for the bone to rebuild itself. Throughout this time, microscopic bone cells repair the break by reorganizing the bone around it and depositing more calcium to make it strong again.

Like the brain, bone is sensitive to the effects of estrogen. In fact, estrogen is critical in maintaining the integrity of bones during a woman's reproductive years. After menopause, the bones of women become very brittle due to the withdrawal of estrogen. This condition, called *osteoporosis*, can lead to life-threatening bone fractures in women after even relatively minor falls or accidents. Tiny fractures in the thin bones of the vertebral column that normally supports the back and keeps us standing tall in an upright position cause loss of height and the development of the unflattering hunchback posture seen in some older women.

As part of the Framingham Study, my colleagues and I measured the bone mineral density (BMD) of more than nine hundred healthy women to see whether the thickness of a woman's bone could predict her chance of getting Alzheimer's disease in the future. A low bone density is a marker of low lifetime estrogen exposure, while a high bone mass suggests high levels of circulating estrogen. After eight years, we found that the women who had the lowest bone density scores had more than twice the risk of developing Alzheimer's disease compared with the women with the highest bone densities.[3] The link between bone density and Alzheimer's disease was strongest when we used measurements taken from the hip bone. One explanation for this is that the hip is composed of a type of bone that is more sensitive to changes in estrogen levels. The findings of this study suggest a correlation between bone and the brain, which we think is due to the unique but complementary effects of circulating estrogen on each organ. In other words, high lifetime exposure to estrogen as suggested by high bone density may help protect the brain from Alzheimer's disease and other forms of memory problems. In contrast, a low bone density, indicative of

3. Tan ZS, Seshadri S, Beiser A, et al. Bone mineral density and the risk of Alzheimer's disease. *Arch Neurol* 2004: in press.

low lifetime estrogen exposures to the bone as well as to the brain, may predispose a person to develop Alzheimer's. More studies are needed to establish this possible link between the bone and the brain. If this association is confirmed, we may be able to identify a woman's risk of developing Alzheimer's disease in the future by simply looking at her bone density scores. And women who have osteoporosis may someday be identified as also having a higher risk of developing memory problems and made prime targets for Alzheimer's preventive measures in conjunction with treatment for their osteoporosis.

NATURAL PLANT ESTROGEN: THE PHYTOESTROGENS

Most women are unaware that the most commonly used estrogen preparations are synthetic and derived from the urine of pregnant mares. In fact, the name of the popular estrogen pill Premarin was coined from the phrase *pregnant mare urine*. Other estrogen preparations are considered natural and taken from plant sources such as soy and yams. There is no scientific evidence that plant-derived estrogens are more effective or safe than those that come from animal sources. But recently, proponents of alternative medicine have proposed the use of plant-derived estrogen as a natural alternative to estrogen pills.

Phytoestrogens are naturally occurring compounds found in many plants, fruits, and vegetables that mimic some of the effects of estrogen on the body. Studies of different populations show that women who regularly take high amounts of phytoestrogens, particularly in the form found in soybean products, have a lower incidence of heart disease, cancers of

> ### *Health Benefits of Plant Estrogens*
>
> Plant estrogens can lower cholesterol, protect against the formation of cancers, and increase the density of bones. Soybeans have been a significant part of the diet in many Asian countries for more than one thousand years and are thought to be responsible for the lower risk of heart disease seen among Asians compared with Western populations. Interestingly, there is also a lower incidence of Alzheimer's disease in countries such as Japan and China.

the breast and uterus, and bothersome menopausal symptoms than those women who follow typical Western diets.[4]

While the connection between phytoestrogens and memory preservation has not been proven, many women have switched from traditional, synthetic estrogen pills to natural plant estrogens to treat symptoms of menopause and have generally found them to be useful for this purpose.[5]

Phytoestrogens come in three different forms:

1. *Isoflavones,* the most potent form of plant estrogens, are found in soybeans, lentils, and chickpeas.
2. *Lignans* are found in flaxseed, grains, lentils, fruits, and vegetables.
3. *Coumestans* are abundant in legumes, especially soybeans.

4. Lissin LW, Cooke JP. Phytoestrogens and cardiovascular health. *J Am Coll Cardiol* 2000;35: 1403–1410.

5. Newton KM, Buist DS, Keenan NL, et al. Use of alternative therapies for menopause symptoms: results of a population-based survey. *Ob Gyn* 2002;100:18–25.

Because of the high demand for plant estrogens, they have been concentrated into pills now sold widely in most health food stores and even over the Internet. Companies that produce and market phytoestrogen pills claim that these compounds are identical to human estrogen and yet completely safe. These claims, as well as the natural occurrence of plant estrogens in food, have led many women to turn to phytoestrogens as an alternative to hormone replacement therapy. While evidence supporting the safety and beneficial effects of plant estrogens is accumulating, we are still several years away from making a definitive recommendation regarding the use of the food or pill form of phytoestrogen instead of traditional, synthetic estrogen pills. The safety of phytoestrogens when taken in high concentrations over long periods of time must also be determined. For now, women who have a personal or a strong family history of breast cancer should think twice before taking large amounts of plant estrogen and do so only under the close supervision of a physician. Taking estrogen pills is not recommended for these women because it may increase the risk of developing malignant breast cancer. Phytoestrogens have estrogen-like activity that may be detrimental to women at high personal or genetic risk for breast cancer. These women should consider other alternative medications that may also be effective in treating menopausal symptoms, including licorice, black and blue cohosh, chasteberry, and evening primrose oil.

THE ESTROGEN BOTTOM LINE

If I had written this book a couple of years ago, I probably would have recommended that women who have no strong contraindications for estrogen should consider taking it to prevent heart disease, treat osteoporosis, control the symptoms of menopause, and even improve their memory. But in light of the results of the groundbreaking Women's Health Initiative,[6] I'm inclined to advise my patients to stay away from long-term estrogen replacement therapy. Specifically, if you have a strong personal history of breast cancer, coronary heart disease, stroke, or blood clots, you should refrain from taking ERT even for short periods of time. But if you have none of these contraindications, and symptoms related to menopause such as hot flashes and emotional lability are bothersome to you, discuss the possibility of going on short-term (six months to four years) estrogen replacement therapy with your physician. To reduce the chance that the symptoms will recur when it comes time to stop estrogen, it should be stopped gradually, omitting one pill a week.

Although estrogen therapy is still the most effective treatment for symptoms of menopause, also consider alternative treatments such as phytoestrogens. Modify your diet to include soybean, grains, fruits, vegetables, and other foods rich in plant estrogens. These naturally occurring plant estrogens are generally safe and may be effective in alleviating menopausal symptoms. Phytoestrogens in concentrated pill forms may also have similar effects. But if you have contraindications for estrogen therapy, bear in mind that the ability of plant estrogens to mimic the good effects of the estrogen hormone may also mean that they have the potential of causing some of the hormone's complications.

6. Shumaker SA, Legault C, Rapp S, et al. Estrogen plus progestin and the incidence of dementia and mild cognitive impairment in postmenopausal women: the Women's Health Initiative Memory Study: a randomized controlled trial. *J Am Med Assoc* 2003;289:2651–2662.

Thanks to the Women's Health Initiative, we now know that estrogen and progesterone combination therapy have no place in disease prevention and may even cause harm rather than good for the body. In the future, it is quite possible that a subset of patients who have a greater-than-average risk of Alzheimer's disease due to lifelong low estrogen exposure as evidenced by low bone density and other markers may be singled out as a group that derives benefits from estrogen therapy despite its other complications. Until then, I do not recommend that women take estrogen to preserve memory, especially when other safer and more effective interventions are available.

PART III

Testing and Preserving Your Mind

As you have learned in previous chapters, good memory requires the seamless cooperation of several distinct mental abilities or cognitive domains. In most cases, forgetfulness can be traced to a failure of one or more of these abilities. In this section, I will introduce you to the Memory Stress Test, an innovative way to test your mind by subdividing it into its component parts:

1. Attention and concentration
2. Language
3. Memory
4. Executive function
5. Abstract thinking
6. Calculation

This test allows you to discover your mind's hidden strengths and weaknesses and to establish your baseline abilities for each cognitive domain. By taking the test periodically, you'll be able to use your performance today as a guide to help you detect and intervene at the earliest sign of a possible problem.

In this section, you will also find the Memory Improvement Program, which includes the Sixty-Minute Brain Workout to keep your mind sharp, as well as practical suggestions on how to make challenging mental tasks of everyday life easier to perform. My Ten Steps to an Age-Proof Mind outline the most crucial steps you should be taking now to make your memory and other mental abilities last a lifetime. Finally, I close by giving you a state-of-the-science view of what to expect from ongoing research searching for preventive strategies and the elusive cure for Alzheimer's disease.

Chapter 10

Stressing the Brain

"The palest ink is better than the best memory."

—CHINESE PROVERB

Consider this scenario: You are running late for an appointment, and the elevator is out of service. You decide to rush up the five flights of stairs to get there. Just after climbing the third flight of stairs, your worsening shortness of breath is suddenly punctuated by a crushing sensation in the center of your chest. You break into a cold sweat and sit yourself down on the floor. Resting there for about ten minutes, you finally catch your breath and the severe chest pain starts easing up. What would you do next?

The answer to this question is probably quite obvious. Most of us would ask the first person we encounter in the stairwell to call an ambulance that would take us to the nearest emergency room. Others may choose to book the first available appointment with their physicians to have their hearts thoroughly checked out. These worrisome symptoms of a coronary heart problem would be enough for your physician to send you for a cardiac stress test. This test involves running on a treadmill with heart monitors connected to your chest as the machine's speed and inclination are progressively increased. Kicking the treadmill's settings up a notch to the next higher level corresponds to an increase in the workload on your heart. The idea is to simulate the cardiac stress of rushing up five flights of stairs or greater while a doctor closely monitors the status of your heart, looking for the warning signs of an impending heart attack.

Consider an alternative scenario: You are running late for your next appointment and the elevator is out of service. You decide to rush up the five flights of stairs to get there. Being physically fit, you manage the stairs without much difficulty, breaking only into a brisk sweat as you get to your destination. As you enter your boss's office, you realize that you have left that all-important report you've been working on for the past week at home, resting on the kitchen table. What would you do next? Besides apologizing or quickly coming up with a creative excuse, most of us would probably do absolutely nothing when our memory fails. While most people are aware that chest pain may herald a heart attack, most are unaware that frequent memory lapses may be heralding the brain attack of Alzheimer's disease.

STRESS TEST FOR THE BRAIN

Recent studies show that much as the heart can be subjected to an exercise or treadmill stress test to bring out otherwise undetectable coronary disease, the brain can be subjected to a cognitive or memory stress test that can bring out incipient memory problems. To carry this out, scientists first tested thirty people ranging in age from forty-seven to eighty-two years for the presence of the ApoE4 allele, a genetic marker that confers an increased risk for Alzheimer's disease. Sixteen of the volunteers were found to be carriers of the gene, while fourteen were not. They all underwent a functional MRI (fMRI) test, which measured the level of activity in different brain areas by detecting subtle changes in cerebral blood flow. The more active a particular brain area was, the higher its blood flow was expected to be. While the fMRI test was being performed, the participants were asked to recall a list of words they had previously been asked to memorize. This simulated the mental stress associated with, say, trying to remember the items in a grocery list you forgot at home. The researchers found that people who were free of Alzheimer's disease but carried its susceptibility gene could recall the word lists just as well as those who didn't have the gene. However, the functional MRI scans of the former group produced signals that were twice as strong and widespread as those found in the latter group. This indicates that the brains of people who were genetically susceptible to Alzheimer's demanded higher degrees of cerebral blood flow for a given amount of mental work. In other words, to accomplish the same task, people at higher risk of getting Alzheimer's need to work twice as hard as normal people.[1]

Two years after the study concluded, the researchers performed memory tests on the people who had the most intense brain signals to determine the trajectory of their intellectual abilities. As predicted, of all the participants in the study, the group whose brains had to work the hardest suffered the

---

1. Bookheimer SY, Strojwas MH, et al. Patterns of brain activation in people at risk for Alzheimer's disease. *N Engl J Med* 2000;343:450–456.

greatest loss in memory ability relative to their baseline performance. The findings of this study, if validated in larger groups of people, have the potential to identify people at high risk of succumbing to Alzheimer's disease even before they show the first sign of a memory problem. As new and more effective ways of preventing the progression of MCI to Alzheimer's are discovered, early identification becomes even more critical since prevention strategies are most effective when applied sooner rather than later.

TESTING YOUR MEMORY

The presence of many types of diseases is detected by the deviation of a certain clinical or laboratory measure over and above a range that is considered "normal." Since human beings are incredibly complex and unique organisms, what is considered normal can vary quite widely among different groups of people. Thus, there is a range of measures that are considered normal for various conditions as defined from studies of large population groups. For instance, a blood pressure measurement that falls between 120/80 and 140/90 is considered normal. A heartbeat somewhere between sixty and one hundred per minute is acceptable. Studies have determined that most people in the population fall within these normal ranges, and that a person who has a measure that deviates significantly beyond these cutoff points on either end of the scale is at an increased risk of disease or other adverse outcomes. Simple instruments can now detect many conditions, such as high blood pressure. Others, like high cholesterol, HIV disease, and diabetes, can be confirmed by relatively simple blood tests. Screening programs can identify people who are in the earliest stages of these diseases, long before any permanent damage occurs.

If a simple blood test or instrument could tell with an acceptable degree of accuracy whether a person has Alzheimer's disease or not, our lives would all be a lot simpler. But the reality is that the brain is far too complex an organ to be tested in this manner. *At present, the only realistic way to determine whether someone is suffering from MCI or Alzheimer's is to administer memory tests.* Although many different types of memory tests are available, they are limited by several factors. One problem is that unlike measuring blood pressure or heart rate, there are no absolute normal and abnormal scores for many memory tests. Normal levels of memory ability vary widely depending on numerous factors, including education, occupation, native intelligence, and test-taking skills. For instance, it is conceivable that a CEO who has MCI might achieve a higher memory test score than a poorly educated mailroom clerk who has an intact memory. This can be explained by the fact that the highly educated executive has taken similar tests in the past, enabling him to perform mental shortcuts that facilitate his arrival at the correct answer despite his mild memory impairments. To account for these differences, the normal scores of standardized memory tests are adjusted based on a person's age and educational attainment. The same scale used to determine the normal memory range for the CEO cannot be used to assess the performance of the mailroom clerk, and vice versa. To illustrate, a score of 74 may be well within the normal range for a person with the clerk's age and educational background, but the same score is considered abnormally low for the executive.

It is virtually impossible to adjust for every single factor that could influence memory abilities. One thing that is especially difficult to adjust for is native intelligence. While age and educational attainment can be easily quantified, intelligence cannot be measured as simply. Native intelligence and memory abilities are just as unique as the people who possess them. Thus, many experts agree that the best way to judge the status of a person's memory and intellectual abilities is to compare these to her own mental performance when she was in her intellectual prime. As you may have surmised, this is only possible if tests of memory and other intellectual functions were administered while she was still intellectually intact. This way, her *cognitive baseline abilities* can be established, recorded, and used to judge the stability or instability of her memory and other mental abilities.

Although some people may have had an IQ test at some point in their lives, I don't know of anyone walking around with his IQ test scores from college in his back pocket. Ideal as it may sound, having every person undergo detailed testing to establish a cognitive baseline is not logistically feasible, but testing and monitoring yourself is. One practical approach to detect early memory problems is to simply monitor your own memory by taking memory tests and being vigilant about any signs of a potential problem. If you suspect that a significant decline in your memory may have occurred, further testing by a memory specialist to confirm or refute this observation can then be performed.

In the following chapter, I will present the Memory Stress Test, which outlines some of the techniques used in my clinic to test someone for the presence of MCI and early Alzheimer's disease. When you take these tests, make sure to jot down and keep your scores regardless of how well or how poorly you do. Your varied scores will help you and your doctor to monitor your mental abilities over time. At some point, your doctor may use your scores in these tests as a guide to establish your past cognitive and memory abilities. This information may no longer be measurable at the time you decide to go for an evaluation and may spell the difference between getting an accurate diagnosis of Alzheimer's disease or not.

Chapter 11

The Memory Stress Test

On the first day of anatomy class back when I was in medical school, I remember standing at the back of a long hallway with my classmates, listening to an elderly professor as she read our group assignments from a piece of paper. One by one, she called out our names and assigned us to random groups of four students each. We did our best to focus our attention on what she was saying, but it wasn't easy. Lined up in neat rows in front of us were cadavers whose outlines we could barely make out under the thick green tarp. When she finished reading our group assignments, the professor told us that over the course of the year, we would get well acquainted with our cadavers. She said that we were about to meet the best teacher we would encounter in medical school.

The dissection of the cadaver was the culmination of our anatomy class. The dead brought new life to the pictures and diagrams we had been studying in our books. The caretakers of the cadavers kept them from decaying in the midst of the course by injecting them with formaldehyde. This provided us with ample time to sequentially dissect the heart, the lungs, the stomach and intestines, the reproductive organs, and the muscles and nerves. Out of respect for the cadaver, we exposed only the part of the body we were studying at the moment, leaving everything else covered. As the end of the year drew closer, curiosity got the best of my group and we decided to sneak a peek at our cadaver's head when the professor wasn't looking. To our surprise, we saw that its skull had been opened and the brain was mysteriously missing. We later learned that the delicate brain had been removed because it could not be preserved inside the skull. The handlers had extracted it soon after death and kept it in preservative-filled jars. There it remained until we were ready to tackle the anatomy of the nervous system.

Having a strong interest in the brain as a medical student, I eagerly awaited the day we were scheduled to study it. When we finally plucked out the three-pound fatty mass from its chemical bath, I was impressed by how remarkably fresh it looked considering that it had been more than six months since its owner died. With scalpels in gloved hands, each member of our group took a turn cutting the brain in the precise fashion dictated by our professor, careful not to accidentally cut a delicate nerve or sever a small artery. With some awe and a lot of confusion, we identified each part of the brain and the function that it controlled. One by one, we examined the brain areas that controlled voluntary movement, those that sensed visual stimuli, and even the horseshoe-shaped mound responsible for short-term memory, the hippocampus. Although the exercise was very informative, I found myself somewhat dissatisfied at the end of it. I had expected that in the process of dissecting the brain we would be able to identify the part that was responsible for some of the human mind's most important functions, such as logical thought, judgment, and emotions. These are the capacities of the mind that distinguish humans from the other animals I had dissected in biology class. But after I had a chance to think it over, my initial bout of disappointment was replaced by a newfound respect for the complexity of the human mind.

Unlike other organs such as the heart, which has a corresponding structure responsible for each function, many of the
functions of the mind cannot be explained by simply dissecting the brain. The mind is an entity whose inner workings remains a mystery to us up to this day.

For years, researchers have struggled to find a way to separate
the worried well from those who are truly in the very early
stages of dementia. While there is no single blood test, brain
scan, or memory test that will confirm the presence or absence
of incipient Alzheimer's disease, it *is* possible to make the diagnosis through a combination of subjective memory complaints
and a battery of objective memory tests. In this chapter, I will
help you to "dissect" the mind into some of the cognitive domains discussed in chapter 2, as well as the mind's other abilities:

1. Attention and concentration
2. Language
3. Memory
4. Executive function
5. Abstract thinking
6. Calculation

I will begin by presenting some of the tests I use in my clinic
to test for memory and other cognitive domains. I invite you
to take these tests and get better acquainted with your mind.

TEST YOUR MIND

The following sets of tests are meant to help you assess your
mind—now and later. By taking these tests and recording
your scores, you are creating a baseline that you can use to

help determine if your memory is stable or declining. Of course, these tests are *not* intended to substitute for a thorough, one-on-one memory evaluation by a trained health professional. A low score or poor performance in these tests *does not* signify that you have a memory problem, just as a high score does not necessarily mean that your mind is intact. This is because performance of these tasks is dependent on several important and highly variable characteristics such as baseline intelligence, level of education, language, and testing conditions. The real value in taking these tests lies in the ability to keep track of your performance over time so that you may determine the stability or decline of your mind. Although there are no restrictions on how often you can take the Memory Stress Test, I suggest that you do so no more often than every four to six months. This way, you can be sure that any improvement in your performance is real, and not due to artificial improvements in scores from practice effects. At the end of the test, I will explain the significance of each section. Do not be discouraged if you find the tests too difficult. They are designed to assess the mental functioning of people with a wide range of abilities. If you have serious concerns about your memory or mental performance, speak to a physician for further evaluation. Many of the questions in this test are best performed with the help of a partner. If none is available at the moment, simply skip those items and go back to them later.

Pick a comfortable, quiet, and well-lit area in your home or office and begin testing your memory.

ATTENTION AND CONCENTRATION

Materials Needed

- **A pen or pencil**
- **Notebook or blank sheets of paper**
- **Stopwatch or timer**

SUBTRACTING EIGHTS

Instructions: Count backward from *one hundred* subtracting by *eight* each time (stop after you reach the fifth number). Take note of the time it takes (in seconds) to accomplish this and write it down. Time limit is ninety seconds.

2. NUMBER LIST FORWARD AND BACKWARD

Instructions:

Part I: Number List Forward

Have someone read each set of numbers to you aloud, pausing one second between each digit. Make sure that each number is read in a slow, monotone voice, and that they are not grouped together. Repeat the numbers in the *correct* order. For example, if a person reads the numbers "eight, five," you say "eight, five." Take note of the number of digits you were able to repeat in the correct order.

```
3-5
2-8-7
9-7-5-3
6-3-4-7-1
8-1-2-9-5-3
5-7-4-2-8-3-6
1-9-7-6-8-4-5-2
```

Part II: Number List Backward

Have someone read each set of numbers to you aloud, pausing one second between each digit. Make sure that each number is read in a slow, monotone voice, and that they are not grouped together. Repeat the numbers in the *reverse* order. For example, a person reads the numbers "eight, five," you say "five, eight." Take note of the number of digits you were able to repeat in the reverse order.

9-6
1-7-5
8-2-4-1
5-6-9-2-8
7-9-1-3-6-2
6-2-5-8-9-1-7
3-9-2-7-4-5-8-1

3. Reversed Months

Instructions: Recite the months of the year backward, starting from December and ending in January. Take
note of the time it takes you to accomplish this
task and write it down. If this task proves too
difficult, name the days of the week backward
instead, starting from Sunday and ending on
Monday. Time limit is ninety seconds.

LANGUAGE

4. PHRASE REPETITION

Instructions: Have someone read each of these phrases to you aloud and repeat them:

a. Methodist Episcopal.
b. No ifs, ands, or buts.
c. Around the block the rugged rabbit ran.
d. She came home in a blue Cadillac and a flood of tears.

5. SENTENCE COMPREHENSION

Instructions: Have someone read you the following questions and write down the answers in your notebook:

a. The big wolf was eaten by the bear holding the monkey. Who stayed alive?
b. Andre is older than Arnel but younger than Abby. Who is the oldest of the three?

Instructions: Have someone read each of these instructions to you and follow them:

c. Put your left hand over your right ear.
d. Point to the ceiling after pointing to the floor.

6. NAMING

Instructions: Ask someone to point out for you common items around the house, while you identify each object by giving its name. Alternatively, open a magazine with lots of pictures and name all the objects in each picture. The following are examples of things that can be used for this purpose:

1. Funnel	11. Celery
2. Cufflink	12. Paper clip
3. Paperweight	13. Dice
4. Lapel	14. Key chain
5. Vase	15. Belt buckle
6. Zucchini	16. Gloves
7. Mustache	17. Sleeve
8. Whisk	18. Fingernail
9. Dominoes	19. Lamp shade
10. Pincushion	20. Pendant

MEMORY

7. VERBAL MEMORY (FOUR-WORD RECALL)

Instructions: Have someone choose one of the following sets of four unrelated words then read each word to you aloud. Make sure that a one-second pause is allowed between words. After committing the words to memory, take note of the time (time zero) and proceed to the next part of the test. After five minutes (from time zero), say the four words out loud and have someone take note of the number of words you remembered correctly. (If you did not remember all the words, have the person read the four words to you again and proceed to the next part of the test.) After ten minutes, say all four words aloud again, and take note of your score. (Again, if your score is less than perfect, have someone read the four words to you one more time.) After thirty minutes, take note of the number of words you remembered correctly:

1. Freedom	Strawberry	Tiger	North
2. Boat	Peter	Wisdom	Pennsylvania
3. Flower	Truck	Valor	Dentist
4. Airplane	Bright	Duck	Forest
5. Lime	Anger	Theater	Spoon

8. VISUAL MEMORY

Instructions: Ask someone to hide five objects around the room while you are watching. You may use common things such as a key, pen, hairbrush, coin, or bills of different denominations. Proceed to the next part of the test. After fifteen minutes, write down the name and location of each object.

EXECUTIVE FUNCTION

9. CLOCK DRAWING

Instructions: Draw a clock, put in all the numbers, and set the hands to ten past eleven.

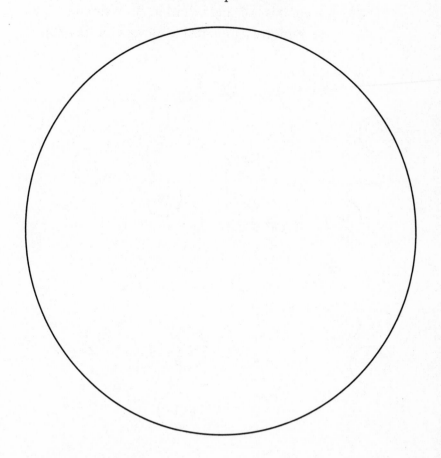

10. TRAIL MAKING TEST A

Instructions: Draw lines to connect the twenty-five consecutively *numbered* circles as fast as you can without lifting the pencil from the paper. Measure the amount of time (in seconds) it takes you to complete this task and record it. A maximum of 120 seconds (two minutes) is allowed for this test.

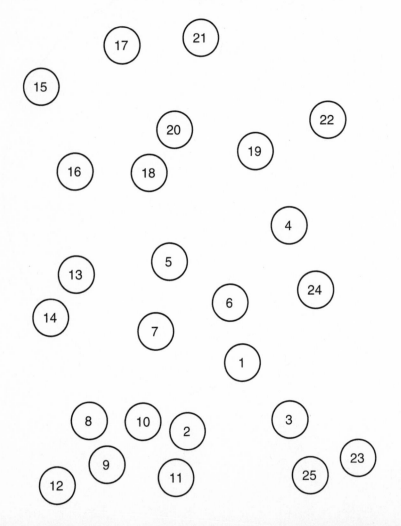

11. TRAIL MAKING TEST B

Instructions: Draw lines to connect the consecutively *numbered* and *lettered* circles, alternating between the two sequences—for instance, 1-A-2-B-3-C, and so on. As in the previous task, draw these lines in sequence as fast as you can without lifting the pencil from the paper and measure the amount of time (in seconds) it takes you to complete it. A maximum of 150 seconds (two and a half minutes) is allowed for this test.

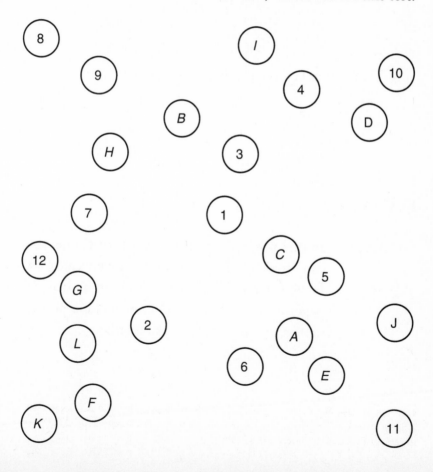

12. WORD LIST GENERATION[1]

Instructions: In one minute, say all the words or things you can think of that begin with the letter specified. Have someone write the words on a sheet of paper as you say them. Do not include proper names (people, places) or different forms of the same word, *(dance, dances, dancing)*, and try not to repeat words.

a. Words that begin with the letter *f*

b. Words that begin with the letter *a*

c. Words that begin with the letter *s*

13. CATEGORY NAMING[2]

Instructions: In one minute, say all the words or things you can think of that fit into the given category. Have someone write the words on a sheet of paper as you say them. Do not include proper names, and try not to repeat words.

1. Benton AL, Hamsher K. *Multilingual Aphasia Examination.* Iowa City: AJA Associates, 1989.
2. Speen O, Strauss E. *A Compendium of Neuropsychological Tests: Administration, Norms and Commentary.* Oxford: Oxford University Press, 1991.

a. Category: Animals

b. Category: Vegetables

c. Category: Fruits

ABSTRACT THINKING

14. PROVERBS

Instructions: In one or two sentences, write down the meaning of these sayings:
   a. Absence makes the heart grow fonder.

   b. People in glass houses should not throw stones.

   c. A penny saved is a penny earned.

15. SIMILARITIES

Instructions: In one or two sentences, write down a characteristic that makes each pair similar. For example: Dog and cat = both are animals.

   a. Apple and pear

b. Poem and sculpture

c. Car and horse

d. Table and chair

CALCULATION

Instructions: Answer the following mathematical questions by performing the calculations in your head. If this is not possible, you may do the calculations on a piece of paper.

16. How many quarters are there in seven dollars and seventy-five cents?

17. If you bought three books for two dollars and seventy-five cents each, and you gave the cashier ten dollars to pay for it, how much change should you expect?

18. I have a total of eighteen books. I want to arrange them such that one shelf has twice as many books as the other. How many books should I put on each shelf?

(End of Test)

Congratulations! Now that you've completed the Memory Stress Test, it's time to find out what each of these questions reveals about your mind. Which areas of your mind are most robust, and which ones require some work to get it to its maximum potential? Below, you will find the answers for each section and an explanation of which cognitive domain each question tested. Read on and find out what a good or fair performance means—and what you should do about it.

ANSWERS AND SCORING

1. 92, 84, 76, 68, 60
2. Number List Forward:

Seven or more	=	Good attention
Five or six	=	Fair attention
Less than five	=	Poor attention

   Number List Backward:

Six or more	=	Good attention
Four or five	=	Fair attention
Less than four	=	Poor attention

   A difference of more than 3 points between forward and backward scores may indicate problems with attention/concentration.
3. A person with good concentration ability should be able to name the months in the following reverse order: December-November-October-September-August-July-June-May-April-March-February-January.
4. Native English speakers should be able to pronounce all the phrases.
5. a. The bear and the monkey.
   b. Abby is the oldest.

    c and d: A person with good comprehension should be able to follow the instructions.

6. A person with good naming ability should not miss more than one or two out of fifteen items.

7. Good memory = Remembers all four words within five minutes and thirty minutes.
Fair memory = Misses one word within five minutes or thirty minutes.
Poor memory = Misses two or more words at five minutes or thirty minutes.

8. Good memory = Remembers all five items and their locations.
Fair memory = Misses one item within fifteen minutes.
Poor memory = Misses two or more items within fifteen minutes.

9. Numbers should be correctly placed and approximately equidistant to each other. The short hand should be pointed past the number 11 and the long hand should be pointed toward the number 2.

10. 25 seconds or less = Good
26–75 seconds = Fair
More than 75 seconds = Poor

11. 75 seconds or less = Good
76–150 seconds = Fair
More than 150 seconds = Poor

12. Twelve words or more per letter = Good
Nine to eleven words per letter = Fair
Eight words or less per letter = Poor

13. Fifteen words or more per category = Good
Eleven to fourteen words or more per category = Fair
Ten words or less per category = Poor

14.[3] a. When a person we love is away, our love for that person increases.
    b. Sensitive people should not throw insults at other people.
    c. Saving money is just as good as earning money.
15.[3] a. Both are fruits.
    b. Both are works of art.
    c. Both are forms of transportation.
    d. Both are types of furniture.
16. Thirty-one quarters.
17. A dollar and seventy-five cents.
18. Twelve books on one shelf, six on the other.

Questions 1–3: Attention and Concentration

Attention is the ability to attend to a task without distraction. Psychologists sometimes liken our mind's attention ability to that of a spotlight used to illuminate actors on a dark stage. All events that are within the beam of light are processed, while events that fall outside it are ignored. A person who has a problem with attention will appear easily distracted and unable to concentrate. Unlike some mental abilities that are localized to one brain area, good attention involves the processing of information sequentially in a series of steps that occur in several different brain areas.

The mind's attention ability has a limited capacity; only so much information can be processed at any one time. Thus, you may be unable to concentrate on a television show while talking

---

3. Other interpretations may also be correct, but the person must recognize the hidden meaning behind the proverbs (refer to the text explanation of Abstract Thinking in this chapter).

to someone on the phone. The term *attention span* refers to the amount of information that a person's mind can hold on to at the same time. The Number List Forward task of the Memory Stress Test is a good test of attention span. It is a relatively effortless task that is not greatly affected by age. A person with good attention should be able to remember at least seven numbers. If you are anxious or distracted by another stimulus, you may remember only five or six numbers even though your attention is normal. In such a situation, I suggest that you take a breather and repeat this part of the test at a later time. If you are still unable to remember at least seven numbers, consider discussing this with your physician.

In contrast to attention span, the term *divided attention* refers to the ability to perform more than one task simultaneously or multiple elements within the same task. These tasks are mentally more taxing, and our skills decline earlier with age and disease compared with tasks that test simple attention span. In the Memory Stress Test, divided attention is tested by the Number List Backward task. The person with good divided attention should be able to mentally manipulate at least five numbers and name them backward. As in the attention span, anxiety or the presence of distractions can impair your ability to perform this task to the best of your ability. However, a consistently low (less than four) score on the Number List Backward task may signal a problem in divided attention. Similarly, a wide discrepancy between Number List Forward and Backward abilities—a difference greater than three—may signal a problem with the mind's attention capacity.

Two other tests, the serial eights and the reversed months, are also tests of attention. The serial subtraction of eight from a hundred additionally requires proficiency in calculation. Someone who has impaired calculation ability will do poorly on this test even though his attention ability is intact. Since everyone knows the months of the year, a person who is able to concentrate should be able to name the months of the year backward without much difficulty. Compared with the other attention tasks, the Reversed Months task is the easiest to perform. Thus, if you are unable to do this even after several trials, speak to your doctor. However, as I mentioned, your attention ability can be affected by anxiety, distractions, physical discomfort, and many other factors. If any of these factors is present, your performance in this section of the Memory Stress Test may not be an accurate representation of your real attention ability. The Sixty-Minute Brain Workout in the next chapter provides specific mental exercises that sharpen attention and concentration abilities. I also offer you some mental techniques and practical tips on how to keep mild problems of attention and concentration from interfering with your daily life. When you take the Memory Stress Test again six months from now, make sure to employ these techniques and see how your score improves.

The Case of Mrs. Glenn

Not too long ago, I got a call from a frantic medical resident who requested me to come to the emergency room ASAP. The patient was an eighty-five-year-old lady who had been brought to the ER after being found strolling the busy streets of Boston in her underwear. She became enraged when she was stopped by a police officer. She even scratched the face of an EMT who tried to take her purse to look for identification.

(continued)

The medical resident was convinced that his patient had either a severe psychiatric problem or, more likely, an advanced form of Alzheimer's disease.

When I saw the poor lady, she was lying on a gurney with a four-point restraint that tethered each extremity to a side rail. The nurse warned me not to get too close, as she was a "spitter." But as I approached, I realized that her mouth was too dry to be any threat. The woman appeared confused but calm. I began by asking her if she knew where she was. She immediately answered that she was in church. I asked her to tell me the year, and she responded, "1905." I requested that she count backward from twenty to one but she just ignored me. Her eyes darted suspiciously from side to side, easily distracted by the people milling about the emergency room.

Realizing that I was unlikely to obtain any information from the patient that night, I excused myself and proceeded to the nurses' station to look at her chart. I dialed her daughter's number; she picked up on the first ring. Marissa painted a very different picture of the mother she'd seen approximately a week before. Mrs. Glenn was a widow who drove, shopped, and lived independently. She even volunteered at the information booth of the local hospital. Marissa could not understand the sudden deterioration in her mother's condition. After I hung up, the medical resident approached me and asked whether I thought Mrs. Glenn had Alzheimer's disease. I told him that I couldn't tell for sure, but chances are she did not. The expression on his face told me he was baffled.

During a memory evaluation, attention is the first thing that I test. This is because a person's ability (or inability) to pay attention is so vital that it taints the results of all other cognitive tests. To be able to follow the test instructions, a person must be attentive and focused. If she is inattentive, it is virtually impossible to make an accurate assessment of her other mental abilities. Thus, before I make a diagnosis of Alzheimer's disease, I first have to make sure that the person's symptoms cannot be explained by an isolated problem with attention.

Mrs. Glenn was not paying attention because she was delirious. *Delirium* is a treatable condition in which a person's attention is compromised by a medical condition and is not directly caused by brain disease. I often see people with delirium in the hospital but refrain from labeling them as having dementia or Alzheimer's disease until the medical condition causing the confusion is treated and cleared. Mrs. Glenn was admitted to the hospital and received intravenous fluids and antibiotics to treat a urinary tract infection. Three weeks later, she was back in her post at the information desk of the hospital. She came in to my clinic for a follow-up a few weeks later. I almost didn't recognize the sweet and soft-spoken woman until I saw her name on the chart. I performed a formal evaluation of her memory and found that her mind was totally intact and free of Alzheimer's disease.

Questions 4–6: Language

The ability to communicate through spoken and written words is one characteristic that distinguishes humans from other animals. Language is a highly complicated skill that is controlled by the higher brain centers of the cerebral cortex. Language and verbal skills continue to develop well into our adult years and even into old age.

The Memory Stress Test evaluates the three primary components of language:

1. Articulation
2. Word comprehension
3. Naming

Repetition of words, phrases, sentences, or even tongue twisters is a good way to check for problems in articulation (the process by which words and syllables are produced to effectively communicate thought). A native English speaker with normal articulation should have no trouble performing the Phrase Repetition tasks of the Memory Stress Test. Make sure that the person reading the phrases reads them to you slowly and clearly, because you can only repeat what you can hear. Difficulty in articulation may be caused by several conditions, including strokes and degenerative brain conditions. If you feel that you may have a problem with articulation, speak to your physician, who may want to do more formal testing to confirm this. These tests might include a CT scan or MRI of the brain to visualize any strokes that have affected the areas of your brain that control language functions.

The second component of language is the ability to understand spoken and written words. This is assessed in the Memory Stress Test by simple word problems and commands such as "Put your right hand over your left eye." The latter test can be adapted to make more versions of the same task by using different body parts, such as "Touch your left elbow to your right thigh." As in the Phrase Repetition task, make sure you hear the question or instruction clearly before you answer or perform it. A person with normal spoken word comprehension should be able to perform these tasks easily. Difficulty in these tasks may reveal a problem with this ability; speak to a physician about further testing. Reading a sentence or paragraph, and writing a sentence, are good ways to evaluate written word comprehension and writing abilities, respectively.

The third component of language is naming. In the Memory Stress Test, asking your mind to retrieve the correct words to match the objects that you are seeing tested your naming ability. Note that naming and other language abilities are affected significantly by many factors, such as educational attainment, primary language, and even cultural background. For instance, several of my Jewish patients could not identify a wreath, and many of my Christian patients could not recognize a menorah. Thus, the person who is choosing objects for you to identify should take this into consideration as well. Assuming that the objects are chosen properly to account for these factors, a person with normal naming ability should be able to identify all but one or two out of fifteen items presented. Problems with naming can be seen in a person who has had a stroke and also those suffering from Alzheimer's disease. If you are concerned about your naming ability, consult your physician for further testing.

Most verbal abilities are resistant to the effects of age. Vocabulary and verbal reasoning abilities remain stable and may even improve in a healthy older person. As I mentioned, however, certain diseases can adversely affect the mind's ability to comprehend and communicate in spoken or written words. Damage to the language center by a stroke can produce profound losses in verbal abilities. Stroke survivors may be unable to use speech to communicate thought. An extreme form of language disability is called *aphasia,* a condition in which the abilities to speak and/or to understand words are completely lost. Other, less serious forms of problems in language include *dysarthria* (difficulty in articulating words) and problems with fluency and reading and writing abilities. Although many diseases can cause language problems, the common experience of occasionally forgetting someone's name or the name of a place we haven't been to for a while does not necessarily signal a serious problem—as long as it doesn't happen repeatedly. If it does, a neuropsychological consultation that formally tests the language ability is in order. In the next chapter, the Sixty-Minute Brain Workout will provide you with some exercises for your language ability. I will also give you some mental techniques that help make remembering names easier and some practical tips on how to keep your language abilities sharp.

Questions 7–8: Memory

Of all of the mind's abilities, memory is arguably the most fascinating and complex. From recognizing the scent of a distinctive perfume to picking out a familiar face in a crowded room, memory takes many different forms and taps several interweaving circuits housed in different parts of the brain. The mind's ability to make, store, and retrieve memory tends to vary widely among people and may even change in the same person depending on certain conditions. It is for this reason that memory is one of the most challenging mental abilities to test.

To get an accurate assessment of the many different types of memory problems, several different forms of memory tests must be administered to a person who shows signs of forgetfulness. To determine the acceptable limits of normal memory, the developers of these tests have given them to large groups of people of various ages and levels of education. Based on this, they have determined a normal cutoff score for each test based on age, education, and other measurable characteristics. A person whose score on a particular test is below this cutoff point is considered to be impaired for the specific type of memory function tested. In this situation, it is still possible for other types of memory abilities to be intact. For instance, a person who cannot recall a list of words he was asked to remember ten minutes ago has a problem with recent memory. But if he is able to remember details of his childhood, he probably has an intact remote memory. Similarly, someone who has difficulty recognizing faces of famous people but can recall most elements of a paragraph she was asked to remember might have a poor visual memory but has a good verbal memory.

The Memory Stress Test examines recent or short-term memory by dividing it into two parts: verbal and visual. The Four-Word Recall task tests your ability to register a set of four unrelated words, and to hold on to them in your memory banks long enough for you to retrieve them five, ten, and thirty minutes later. A person with an excellent memory will remember the four words very easily at five minutes. In fact, she can probably recall even a string of five, six, or even seven words without much difficulty. I purposely limited the word recall task to four words to account for differences in baseline memory abilities. The vast majority of people will be able to remember all four words, while a minority will forget one out of four words five minutes after these are first read to them. After the words are repeated to people belonging to the latter group, they should be able to remember all four words ten minutes later through the process of *learning*. If at thirty minutes after the third repetition of the list, the person is still unable to remember all four words, a problem with learning and memory may exist. These people, and those who are convinced they have a memory problem but find these tests too easy given their high intelligence or educational attainment, should ask their physician for a neuropsychological test.

The test for visual memory also evaluates short-term memory and may be a more appropriate test for people with language problems and those with low educational attainment. Unlike the test for verbal memory described above, it does not require familiarity with words. The Memory Stress Test's Visual Memory task involves having someone hide five objects around the room while you are watching and then trying to recall which object is hidden where after fifteen minutes. In my clinic, I find that hiding paper bills of different denominations is particularly effective for people who are disinterested in being tested, probably because of the almost universal importance attached to money. A person with good memory will remember all the items, while those with fair memory will remember all but one item. Forgetting more than one item may indicate a problem with visual memory. However, remember that anxiety, the presence of distractions, and other factors may interfere with your best memory performance. Consult your physician if you are concerned about your visual memory ability.

For a more detailed discussion of the whys and hows of normal memory and forgetfulness, please refer to the discussion in part 1. In the next chapter, I will present some proven mental techniques that will help you remember; in the Sixty-Minute Brain Workout, I will provide you with exercises you can use to practice your memory abilities.

Questions 9–13: Executive Function

An independent life demands that people be able to perform a complicated series of functions allowing them to survive in an increasingly demanding and competitive society. Exercising good judgment, engaging in useful work, maintaining social relationships, and performing self-care functions are just some of the activities that are essential for independent living. *Executive function* refers to the ability to plan and perform tasks in sequence and the mental flexibility to shift from one task to another. To be able to work as a taxi driver, for instance, you need to have a good memory to remember each passenger's destination, pay attention to other cars on the road, be well oriented to the layout of the city to find the quickest route, and remain mentally flexible to alter the original route in case of unexpected detours or traffic jams. As you might deduce, the performance of these complicated functions involves the interaction of several different brain areas. Consequently, damage to any one of these brain areas will result in an impairment of this mental ability.

The human mind's executive function is really composed of four distinct but closely linked stages, namely:

1. Volition
2. Planning
3. Purposive action
4. Effective performance[4]

Tests that tap into one or more of these stages bring out any underlying defects in executive function. Thus, the Memory Stress Test presents several tests that require varying degrees of planning and mental flexibility. The Clock Drawing task is a popular test that assesses not only executive function but also other important mental abilities. It is sometimes used as a screening test for people suspected of having Alzheimer's disease. When the person is instructed to draw a clock, put in all the numbers, and set the hands of the clock to ten past eleven, the task should be well executed, with the numbers in the right positions and the hands placed approximately correctly. Although a person with an intact mind may find this a rather simple task, it really requires complex interactions among the mind's visual construction skill, executive function, attention, number-processing, and number–time relationship understanding abilities. Common mistakes include poor planning that results in irregular placement of the numbers, or misinterpreting the instructions and literally setting the hands of the clock such that one is pointing to the number 10 and the other to 11 ("ten past eleven"). Either of these may point to a problem in executive function. The Clock Drawing task can be adapted by changing the instructions on the placement of the hands to say, "five minutes to eight" or "fifteen past two."

Other tests for executive function are the Trail Making Tests A and B (questions 10 and 11). These tests were origi-

4. Lezak MD. *Neuropsychological Assessment*, 3rd ed. New York: Oxford University Press, 1995.

nally developed by U.S. Army psychologists in 1944 to test soldiers who suffered head trauma in battle. They are now among the best-known tests for executive function. Test A simply requires you to draw lines to connect consecutively numbered circles on a sheet of paper. A person with excellent executive function will be able to complete this task in twenty-five seconds or less, while most people will be able to complete it in one minute and fifteen seconds. Trail Making Test B is similar but requires you to alternate between two sequences (number and letter) and is therefore more challenging. It should take no more than two and a half minutes to complete this task, and most people will finish well before this. Both tests require visual scanning, planning, attention, and good motor agility. Slow or inaccurate performance of either test may point to a problem in any or all of these abilities. If it takes you longer than a minute and fifteen seconds to complete Trail Making Test A or longer than three minutes to perform Trail Making Test B, a problem with executive function may exist. Also, when the time required to complete Trail Making Test B is more than two minutes over that needed to complete Trail Making Test A, you may have problems with attention that appear only when performing a single complex task or several tasks at the same time (multitasking). Strokes and degenerative conditions such as Alzheimer's can lead to poor executive function ability.

Executive function problems manifest themselves in different ways. Some people may find it challenging to organize and perform tasks in the correct sequence, such as following a medication schedule or a recipe. Others may experience difficulty in self-control, manifesting as socially inappropriate behavior like urinating in public or other bizarre behaviors as in the case of Dr. Alan Zarkin, who carved his initials on his patient's belly. People with executive function problems can become impulsive, careless, easily irritable, and excitable. They can become poorly motivated to engage in self-care activities such as grooming and bathing, leading to poor personal hygiene. Due to its peculiar presentation, people suffering from executive dysfunction are sometimes misconstrued by friends and relatives as being lazy or even psychiatrically disturbed. Simple mental tests, similar to the ones presented in the Memory Stress Test, can reveal gross abnormalities in the mind's executive function and judgment. If you feel that you or someone you know may have a problem with executive function, speak to a physician about it to see if further testing is appropriate. The Sixty-Minute Brain Workout in the next chapter presents several exercises that require mental flexibility. I will also provide you with some practical tips on how to minimize the effects of poor executive function in your daily life.

Questions 14–15: Abstract Thinking

Broadly defined, *abstract thinking* is simply the ability to grasp a concept with mental flexibility and the capacity to resist concrete thinking. To illustrate, most people recognize that the proverb "A rolling stone gathers no moss" has more than one meaning. A person who has a defect in abstract thinking or concept formation can only grasp the literal interpretation of the phrase: No moss will grow on a stone that is rolling. Although not necessarily wrong, this *concrete* interpretation of the statement is the product of an inflexible mind. The "hidden" meaning of the proverb requires a bit of mental flexibility to decipher. A common *abstract* interpretation of this proverb is that "a person who keeps on moving will not have anything." The ability to give this alternate and less concrete interpretation of the same statement depends on the integrity of several of the mind's abilities, including good and accessible memory stores, intact interconnections among several different brain areas, and the capacity to process two or more mental events at one time. Because abstract thinking and concept formation demand the interaction of several brain areas, injury to different parts of the brain can give rise to mental inflexibility.

One thing that distinguishes abstract thinking from other cognitive domains is its selective focus on the *quality* and *process* of thinking rather than on the *content* of the answer. That is, if I asked you to tell me the correct change from a dollar after purchasing three items that cost fourteen cents each, I am really interested more in finding out whether you are able to come up with the correct answer than in the mathematical formula you use to get to it. In contrast, if I ask you to interpret the proverb "A bird in the hand is better than two in the bush," I'm more interested in how you arrive at the answer than the answer itself. This is because many tests of abstract thinking do not have only one correct interpretation. In fact, most of them have several acceptable meanings. Thus, the examiner must make a qualitative judgment of whether a person's interpretation of a proverb is abstract or concrete and whether it is apt or irrelevant.

The Memory Stress Test presents several proverbs that may have several interpretations. Proverb tests are a good way to assess mental flexibility in older people who grew up in a generation where these sayings were part of everyday language. Younger people who are unfamiliar with proverbs may find it more difficult to interpret them, not because they have a problem with abstract thinking but more because they simply have never heard them before. Thus, people belonging to a younger generation may do better with the tests of similarities

A Special Note on Reasoning

To reason is to comprehend relationships, think logically, and exercise practical judgments. Like tests for abstract thinking, reasoning tests have no one "right" or "wrong" answer. More important to the examiner than the answer is the thought process that led to it. Reasoning ability can be tested in verbal or visual forms. Verbal reasoning tests comprehension by asking questions that are answerable by practical reasoning and commonsense judgment. Proverb interpretation tests can be used for this purpose. Visual reasoning requires logical explanation or completion of a problem presented in picture form. In the picture completion test of visual reasoning, a person is instructed to complete a picture by drawing in the missing component. For example, a picture of a guitar missing the strings can be presented; the person being tested is expected to draw the missing strings to complete the guitar picture. Alternatively, the person is asked to rearrange a series of related pictures to tell a logical visual story. Reasoning ability is one of the most difficult to test because it requires that the examiner exercise subjective judgment of whether the person is thinking and reasoning logically or not. Thus, a complete test of reasoning ability is best performed by a trained psychologist and has not been included in the Memory Stress Test.

and differences. Like the proverbs, these tests may have more than one correct answer. The best way to determine whether your performance in either of these tests is normal or not is to ask another person whether the answer you gave is one that he would expect a reasonable person to give. For instance, when asked how a pear and apple are alike, most people would state that they are both fruits. However, it would also be acceptable if someone says that they are both edible. A problem with abstract thinking usually does not occur in isolation; by the time this mental ability is affected by a disease such as Alzheimer's, other cognitive domains are typically involved as well. Thus, if you did well with the other parts of the Memory Stress Test but encountered difficulty with the tests of abstract thinking, your mind is probably okay. As is true for the other parts of the test, if you are concerned about this mental ability, speak to your physician about it.

Questions 16–18: Calculation

Calculation is really a form of reasoning using numbers instead of words and sentences. But unlike tests of verbal and visual reasoning, most tests of calculation have only one right answer. The tests for this skill come in a variety of forms, from simple arithmetic problems to more complicated word problems similar to the ones we wrestled with in high school algebra class. They are very sensitive to the effect of education, such that highly educated people are expected to perform significantly better than those with less schooling. In general, men tend to outperform women and whites tend to have higher scores than blacks in mathematical tests. In addition to reasoning ability, coming up with the solution to a mathematical problem requires an intact memory to apply arithmetic rules, and good concentration to mentally manipulate the numbers. If either the memory or concentration ability is defective, calculation becomes similarly compromised.

In the Memory Stress Test, I presented several mathematical problems that can be performed mentally by most people. Someone with at least a high school level of education should be able to come up with the correct answers. However, people with less than a high school education or those who have struggled with math even when they were young should be allowed to use a pen and paper to come up with the correct answers. A person who once had good mathematical abilities and who now finds it difficult to balance a checkbook or perform simple mathematical calculations should be referred to a neuropsychologist for an evaluation of this and other cognitive domains. Like problems with abstract thinking, calculation problems do not usually occur in isolation. Thus, if you encounter difficulty in performing the mathematical problems in the Memory Stress Test but do well in all the other sections, don't worry. Chances are, your memory is just fine. Calculation is a skill, and as with any other skill, lack of practice due to lifelong dependence on mental crutches such as calculators and computers can make it rusty. In the next chapter, I provide you with some practical tips on how you can resharpen this skill in the course of your daily life.

The Case of Joshua Applebaum

Joshua Applebaum worked as an accountant in Brooklyn for more than forty years. He handled the books of several delis, butcher shops, and convenience stores so well that his clients continued to look to him to do their taxes even after they had retired and moved out of the area. He had clusters of loyal clients in cities all across the eastern seaboard, extending as far south as Miami Beach and as far north as Kennebunkport, Maine. At the end of a particularly busy tax season, he saw me for what his wife referred to as "befuddlement." It began when Mrs. Applebaum received a phone call from Rabbi Ginsburg, one of her husband's clients in a retirement community in Naples, Florida. The rabbi thought it was odd that it took his old friend more than four hours to do his taxes when it used to take him no more than an hour to do so. He investigated by secretly watching Mr. Applebaum as he worked. He confirmed his suspicion that something was amiss when the man who used to do complicated tax calculations in his mind pulled out a calculator from his old briefcase.

When I questioned Mr. Applebaum about this, he sheepishly confessed that he had been relying on a calculator for the past three tax seasons. He had successfully avoided embarrassment by secretly using the calculator only after his clients had left him alone in a room. Initially, only large numbers bothered him. But lately, he had found it a challenge to remember even basic arithmetic rules. I gave him a simple math problem: "6 + 8 − 3." It took him about a minute, but he

(continued)

eventually came up with the correct answer. Mrs. Applebaum gave an audible sigh of relief. Next, I gave him a slightly more challenging problem: "How many nickels are there in two dollars and thirty-five cents?" He tried to figure it out in his head but after about two minutes he politely asked if he could use a pen and paper. After scribbling a series of illegible numbers, he finally gave me an incorrect answer of twenty-three nickels. Mr. Applebaum clearly had problems with calculation. This was even more pronounced considering his occupation and his mind's previously superior calculation ability. Upon further testing, it became evident that this was not his only problem; he also had trouble with memory and executive function. I gave him a diagnosis of Alzheimer's disease and started him on medications to treat this problem. He retired from accounting after the diagnosis, but he continues to balance his checkbook with the aid of his calculator and the watchful eye of Mrs. Applebaum.

ORIENTATION

We commonly use the word *orientation* to refer to the position of a certain thing in space—the southeast orientation of a street, for example. But in psychology, this term means something slightly different. Orientation is a person's awareness of the self in relation to the surroundings. Good orientation demands that a person be attentive, be perceptive, and have a good memory. This means that like other mental abilities, orientation is reliant on the cooperation of several different brain areas, and that a problem in any one of these will lead to disorientation. In fact, problems with orientation are among the most common manifestations of the later stages of a brain disease. Normal orientation implies awareness in the three different domains of time, place, and person. Of these, disorientation to time and place are most frequent. Unlike orientation to person, time and place change constantly and demand continuous awareness of the surroundings and the translation of immediate experiences into meaningful memories.

An intact orientation does not necessarily mean that a person's memory and other cognitive functions are normal. Mild defects in attention and memory do not usually manifest as disorientation. Thus, orientation to time, place, and person are usually intact in people with MCI and early Alzheimer's disease. It is only in the moderate to late stages of the disease that problems with orientation become evident. It is not unusual for someone suffering from moderate to advanced Alzheimer's disease to get up and get dressed at 3 A.M. because the mind has lost its sense of orientation to time and cannot distinguish between day and night. Disorientation to place leads to wandering behavior and, consequently, the risk of getting lost. But for family members, the most heartbreaking event occurs when their loved ones finally lose their orientation to person. When parents with Alzheimer's fail to recognize their own sons, daughters, grandchildren, and even lifelong partners, the pain becomes almost unbearable.

It has become routine for physicians to test for orientation during an evaluation of a patient's mental status. Questions that test a person's orientation to time, place, and personal data such as age, name, marital status, date of birth, and number of children are essential. Requesting a person to name the day, month, year, day of the week, and time of day are also good tests of orientation to time. Asking a person to name the location she is in, such as the city, county, and state or the floor of the building, can assess orientation to place. To evaluate orientation to person, have her identify the president of the country, the vice president, and the governor of the state. Asking a person to identify family members and friends in pictures is also a good way to test orientation to person. Because the correct answers to tests of orientation tend to vary widely depending on a person's particular life situation, I decided not to include this in the Memory Stress Test. Instead, I have provided you with an example of another test that primarily tests this mental ability.

THE SHORT PORTABLE MENTAL STATUS QUESTIONNAIRE (SPMSQ)

The Short Portable Mental Status Questionnaire (SPMSQ) is a screening test for the adequacy of intellectual function in older people. I've included it here to show you an alternate way that orientation, memory, and other mental abilities can be tested. It is much shorter than the Memory Stress Test but also less comprehensive. Out of the ten questions, seven require good orientation to answer correctly. It asks the person to identify the date, the day of the week, the address, and other tests of orientation. It is specifically designed for people older than sixty-five who, because of a low educational attainment or a language barrier, may find the Memory Stress Test too challenging. A person with a high school education should make no more than one or two mistakes in the

Short Portable Mental Status Questionnaire (SPMSQ)

Patient's Name: _____   Date: _____

Circle One: SEX: M F   RACE: White Black Other   YRS OF EDUCATION: Grade School   High School   Beyond High School

Instructions: Ask questions 1 to 10 on this list and record all answers. (Ask Question 4a only if the subject does not have a telephone.) Record the total number of errors based on the answers to the 10 questions.

+	–	Questions	Instructions
		1. What is the date today?	Correct only when the month, date, and year are all correct.
		2. What day of the week is it?	Correct only when the day is correct.
		3. What is the name of this place?	Correct if any of the description of the location is given. "My home," the correct city/town or the correct name of the hospital/institution is acceptable.
		4. What is your telephone number?	Correct when the number can be verified or the subject can repeat the same number at a later time in the interview.
		4a. What is your street address?	Ask only if the subject does not have a telephone.
		5. How old are you?	Correct when the stated age corresponds to the date of birth.
		6. When were you born?	Correct only when the month, date, and year are correct.
		7. Who is the president of the United States now?	Requires only the correct last name.
		8. Who was president just before him?	Requires only the correct last name.
		9. What was your mother's maiden name?	Needs no verification; it only requires a female first name plus a last name other than the subject's.
		10. Subtract 3 from 20 and keep subtracting 3 from each new number, all the way down.	Any error in the series—or an unwillingness to attempt the series—is scored as incorrect.

_____ Total Number of Errors

- 0–2 errors = Intact Intellectual Function
- 3–4 errors = Mild Intellectual Function
- 5–7 errors = Moderate Intellectual Function
- 8–10 errors = Severe Intellectual Function

(Allow one more error for a subject with only a grade school education. Allow one less error for a subject with education beyond high school. Allow one more error for African American subjects using identical educational criteria.)

Source: Pfeiffer E. A short portable mental status questionnaire for the assessment of organic brain deficit in elderly patients. J Am Ger Soc 1975 Oct;23(10):433–441.
Reprinted with permission: Blackwell Publishing Ltd.

SPMSQ. Note that as a brief screening instrument, the SPMSQ may be completely normal in people with early memory impairment. Like the Memory Stress Test, it is not meant to diagnose or exclude the presence of memory problems. However, if a person has a good performance on the SPMSQ today but does poorly on it months or years from now, a problem may be brewing and a more thorough evaluation by a physician may be appropriate.

SAVING YOUR MENTAL ABILITIES

The Memory Stress Test has provided you with several ways to get acquainted with your mind's strengths and perhaps even some of its weaknesses. This snapshot of your mind's current level of functioning is important today but may even be more valuable in the future. If you ever find a need to have a more thorough memory assessment, you will find that the tests used by the neuropsychologist is very similar to the ones presented here. Make sure to record and save your scores each time you perform the test. Although the Memory Stress Test can be taken as often as necessary, I again advise allowing at least six months between administrations to avoid artificial improvements in performance that are attributable to practice effects. If you have any concerns about the status of your memory after performing any of the tests, make sure to speak to your physician, who will be in the best position to judge whether further testing is necessary.

Now that you have identified your cognitive strengths and weaknesses (and will continue to as you test your mind again and again), you can move on to the Memory Improvement

Program. This comprehensive program designed to sharpen your mind includes mental techniques to help you remember better, a Sixty-Minute Brain Workout program to keep your mind sharp, and practical tips on how to keep your mental weaknesses from interfering with your daily life. I encourage you to take note of which parts of the Memory Stress Test you didn't do as well on, and the corresponding mental ability they represent. You can then use this knowledge as a guide when you move on to the next chapter to help you decide if you need to concentrate your efforts in strengthening a specific mental ability, or if a general memory improvement strategy is more appropriate.

Chapter 12

The Memory Improvement Program

"Lord, keep my memory green."
—CHARLES DICKENS

Studies have shown that certain memory improvement techniques have the capacity to delay or even reverse the memory declines that occur with age.[1] In fact, these strategies can improve the memory performance of older adults even into very old age. The ability to remember names and faces, appointments, and supermarket or medication lists are just some of the everyday tasks that can be enhanced by following the simple but powerful strategies that will be presented in this chapter. The mental techniques include *visualization* (seeing with your mind's eye), *association* (combining two or more things), *method of loci* (placing things sequentially in a familiar mental route), and *chunking* (grouping things together into larger memory bits). In the next sections, I will describe how to

1. Saczynski JS, Rebok GW. Strategies for memory improvement in older adults. *Top Adv Practice Nursing* 2004;4(1).

use these and other techniques and give you specific examples of their application. After you become comfortable with these techniques, I will then introduce you to the Sixty-Minute Brain Workout, a set of mental exercises especially developed for this book to provide you with a way to keep your mind sharp. I will also give you some practical tips on how to better and more easily perform everyday memory tasks such as remembering to keep important appointments, following medication schedules, and even recalling where you left your keys.

I will be the first to admit that while the mental techniques I will present here are quite simple to learn, their initial application to everyday situations is not intuitive. In fact, some people may even find some of the strategies to be quite tedious at first. Then again, what effective workout program isn't? Much like a physical exercise workout program, the memory workout can be challenging in the beginning. But those who stick with the program and practice the techniques regularly are the ones most likely to reap the greatest rewards of a better memory when they need it most. To begin, let's discuss the first of two global memory improvement strategies.

REMEMBERING BY VISUALIZATION

Global memory improvement strategies are techniques that can be applied to a wide variety of memory tasks. *Visualization* is one such strategy. It is the process of seeing with the "mind's eye" the thing that you are trying to remember. Creating a mental picture of an object gives it meaning and facilitates later recall. Visualization ensures that the mind has acknowledged that something needs to be remembered and creates visual understanding of an object. To illustrate, let's say you were asked to remember an important list of five unrelated things. Committing these to memory and later recalling them takes a significant amount of mental effort. But by investing time to apply the visualization technique, you can paint a striking mental picture that ties all of the objects together into one logical (or illogical) whole. In so doing, you have drastically reduced the amount of work your mind needs to expend to recall the word list later.

Mrs. Jameson's Technique

I had been testing Theresa Jameson's memory for the past thirty minutes, and she'd had just about enough of it. Mrs. Jameson was an exceptionally intelligent lady. After graduating with the highest honors from Wellesley College, she chose to marry her high school sweetheart and stay at home to raise their four children. At the age of forty-eight, after her youngest child went off to college, Mrs. Jameson decided to go back to school herself. Before long, she had earned a doctorate in education and was tutoring a handful of children with learning disabilities in her Cambridge home. Her reputation as an excellent and innovative teacher swiftly spread beyond her neighborhood, and twenty years later she was the principal of the largest school for special-needs students in southeastern New England. Her daughter Jessica worked as a teacher in the school and was well aware of her mother's intelligence. Thus, when she noticed that Mrs. Jameson had begun having difficulty remembering the names of the children, she became worried. She knew that her mother would be resistant to having any kind of memory evaluation. Thus, she told her that she was coming in for a physical checkup. Mrs. Jameson became visibly upset when she later found out that her daughter had tricked her into getting a memory checkup instead. She threatened to leave but reluctantly agreed to stay after her daughter tearfully informed her that her brothers and sisters shared her concerns.

As part of the evaluation, I asked her questions designed to test the limits of her memory. Proud of her intelligence, Mrs. Jameson initially felt slighted when I asked her questions that she considered too simple. "Even my first-graders know the answers to those silly questions!" But as the questions became more challenging, her demeanor drastically changed. Anger and denial are defense mechanisms commonly employed by people in the early stages of a memory problem. When I noticed that she was becoming irritable whenever she felt unsure of the answer, I assured her that she was doing well and promised to end the testing after one last set of tests. I read her a list of five unrelated words—*fish, shirt, ball, mirror, lake*—and asked her to remember it. She closed her eyes for half a minute, as if trying to picture the words in her mind. When she finally opened her eyes, I asked her to repeat the words to me. With confidence, Mrs. Jameson told me the words in the exact sequence and pace I had read them to her. I distracted her by making her draw a clock and name some pictures, yet she remembered all the words even after twenty minutes had elapsed. At the end of the examination, I asked her

(continued)

how she had remembered all the words so effortlessly. She smiled for the first time since I'd met her and said that she simply applied some of the techniques she had taught her learning-disabled students over the years. She visualized a fish wearing a baseball shirt using the surface of the lake as a mirror. This made recalling the list of words quite a breeze.

Visualization is a powerful strategy of memory enhancement, but it may not come easily for some people. Like any new technique, it requires regular practice until it can be applied relatively effortlessly in everyday life. To illustrate the effectiveness of visualization, try to think of the total number of windows you have in your house. Most people will find this a challenging task. But if you mentally visualize yourself walking through the front door of your house and methodically going from room to room, you will likely find this difficult task much easier. There is no one right or wrong way of applying the visualization technique of remembering things. For the life of me, I could not have predicted that Mrs. Jameson's would be a mental picture of a fish dressed in a baseball shirt. But through her imagination, she conjured up this rather odd picture, which made the words all that easier to remember. When applying the visualization technique, allow your imagination to run wild. The more unusual the mental picture, the more unforgettable it is likely to be. For instance, to help you remember a doctor's appointment at 3 P.M., you can visualize a big tree growing at the center of the waiting area of the clinic. This strange mental picture will make it highly unlikely for you to forget to show up for this important appointment.

Also, to help you recall that you parked your car in garage area 4b, simply visualize four honeybees circling your car. Although it can be used alone, the visualization technique is most powerful when it is combined with the strategy I will be discussing next: the technique of association.

REMEMBERING BY ASSOCIATION

In addition to visualization, Mrs. Jameson also applied the second global memory improvement strategy, known as the *association* technique. This strategy involves the combination of two or more things that you want to remember in a meaningful way. The association technique is typically used to remember two or more unrelated words. It is most effective when used along with the visualization technique just described. As in visualization, a strange association is typically easier to remember than an intuitive one. For instance, to help me remember to pick up a quart of milk and two pounds of salmon on the way home, I find a creative way to combine these two unrelated things visually. Through the association technique, I will picture myself opening the trunk of my car and finding it filled with milk, with a two-pound salmon swimming gracefully in it. Thus, when I put my briefcase in the trunk on my way home, the strange image will pop in my mind and I will remember to pass by the supermarket and pick up those two items. Note that adding motion to the picture makes it more dynamic and that much harder to forget.

As an exercise, take a minute to try to remember the following list by using the association technique:

Book
Chocolate
Moon
Car
Tiger

Now put the book away and write down all the words on the list using the mental picture you just created to help you recall the words. For me, the mental picture was that of a tiger riding a car made of chocolate on the surface of the moon while trying to read a book. What was yours?

Practice is the key to mastering these global memory improvement strategies. Next time you are reading a newspaper, try to pick out two or more unrelated words at random and apply the visualization and association techniques to see for yourself how these strategies can help you remember things a lot easier.

THE TASK-SPECIFIC MEMORY IMPROVEMENT STRATEGIES

Now that you are familiar with the global memory improvement techniques of visualization and association, let's move on to the task-specific memory strategies of method of loci, chunking, and name–face recall. These strategies make use of the global techniques to help out your memory in specific situations, such as remembering long grocery lists, the names and faces of new acquaintances, and important dates or numbers. Make sure that you are comfortable with visualization and association before you proceed, because you will be asked to apply these techniques extensively in the task-specific memory strategies that follow. If you are ready, go on to the next section to learn about the first strategy that will help you remember a list of words or objects.

Remembering by the Method of Loci

The first of the task-specific memory improvement techniques is called the *method of loci*. This visualization technique uses a route so familiar to you that it is almost automatic—perhaps a route you have taken from home to work for many years or even a work routine you have followed throughout your career. Along this route, the items to be remembered are mentally placed for easier learning and recall later. The method of loci technique is particularly useful in remembering long lists of words such as supermarket lists or a list of things to do for the day.

The first step in using this powerful strategy is to choose a route that you are very familiar with. I use the subway stops on my way home as my personal memory route. Except for several days during the peak winter months when it is too cold to walk, I take the subway to and from work every day. Thus, I have become intimately familiar with the stops that the E train makes along the green line of the T, the local moniker for the Boston metro-area subway system. In fact, I am so familiar with the route and the approximate amount of time it takes the train to get from work to home that I never miss a stop even if I doze off on the train after a long day preceded by a busy night on call. For this reason, I chose these stops as the route I use to remember important lists.

I usually get on the train at the Brigham Circle T stop, which is conveniently located just across the street from the medical school on Huntington Avenue. From there, it makes stops in several Boston landmarks: the Longwood medical area, the Museum of Fine Arts, Northeastern University, Symphony Hall, Prudential Center . . . Using this as my route, I visualize each item I want to remember and associate it with one specific stop. For instance, this weekend I am planning to do the laundry, pick up stamps from the post office, pay the bills, return a book to the library, and call my parents. To make sure I don't forget to do these things, I visualize a line of white trucks picking up laundry from the hospital, the marquee of the museum announcing an exhibit of rare stamps, the central green of the university strewn with books, my parents playing cello and trombones with the Boston Symphony Orchestra, and a pile of unpaid shopping bills as tall as the fifty-two-story Prudential tower. Of course, I could have used other routes or routines that are personally meaningful to me. All of us can think of something that is so automatic to us that our brain hardly needs to do any work to remember it. Something as simple as your morning routine (turn off the alarm clock, turn on the coffeemaker, hop into the shower, brush your teeth . . .) or the parts of the body (hair, forehead, eyes, ears, nose, mouth, chin, neck, shoulders . . .) can be effectively used for this purpose. You may want to begin with five to seven locations and expand or shorten it depending on your ability and comfort level. The important thing is to acknowledge your chosen route or routine by visualizing each step or location. Once you can name each step effortlessly, practice using the method of loci strategy when trying to remember any list. This could be a list of names of people you are planning to invite to a party, the list of gifts you need to pick up for family members, or the list of appointments you have for the day or week.

Remembering Names and Faces

When I was a young man, I realized that remembering names and faces was not my greatest mental ability. Although I could recognize the face of almost any person I met, I found it challenging to associate their names with their faces. I didn't realize why until much later when I read about the theories on the different ways that people learn. According to the learning-style theory of adult learning, some people are *tree learners* while others are *forest learners.* Forest learners remember things by looking at the big (overall) picture first before tackling the individual (smaller) parts that make up the big picture. Such people are also called *global learners* because of their uncanny ability to process multiple bits of information simultaneously. They are thought to learn primarily through their right brain. In contrast, tree learners (also called *analytic learners*) primarily use the left brain for processing new information. They prefer to process information logically and sequentially. Tree learners are linear thinkers who look at the individual (smaller) parts first before considering the big picture that arises from them.

Of course, no one learns purely by just one method. As learners, we all fall somewhere in between these two extremes, but probably very few are truly in the middle. Most of us lean toward either forest learning or tree learning. I am more of a forest learner. I prefer looking at the big picture first before focusing on its smaller component parts. This learning style is probably why I found it a challenge to associate names with faces. I had to make a conscious effort to become a tree learner in this situation.

As they grow older, even tree learners can encounter problems trying to remember the name or face of a person they have not seen for a while. This is when the name–face association strategy can help. This strategy involves the association of a prominent feature of a person's face (a large nose, a small mouth, a wide forehead) with their name to facilitate later recall. This technique forces forest learners to look for a small but prominent part of a person's appearance and find a way to associate it with his name. Of course, not every person we meet will have a prominent feature that we can use to associate his name with. In such instances, it is useful to visualize the person in a situation that you can associate with a distinctive feature of his name. For example, I once met a landscape contractor named Richard Goldstone. I visualized him as being so rich that he had stones made of gold in his garden. Alternatively, you can associate a person's first or last name with a familiar person or a celebrity that she may vaguely resemble. Pick any one or more of these techniques to better remember names the next time you go to a party or meet a new client, and see what best works for you.

Remembering by Chunking

Many people are already experts at applying an effective memory strategy called *chunking* without knowing it. Whenever we try to remember a phone number or an important date by breaking the individual digits up into smaller, more manageable "chunks," we are inadvertently practicing this technique. The common strategy of remembering a string of numbers such as 6174324807 by breaking it up into smaller units like 617-432-4807—as we customarily do with telephone numbers—is the chunking technique at work. But this strategy can be used in many other types of memory tasks, such as remembering a medication list by chunking them according to their indication: blood pressure medicines, diabetes medicines, heart medicines, and so on. The chunking technique can also be supplemented with the global strategy of association to make each chunk more meaningful and easier to recall. For instance, my brother Ted's birthday is May 26, 1964. To remember the date 5-26-64, I try to associate each chunk with something memorable that will help me recall it. In this case, 5 is the number of siblings in our family, 26 was the age that I started residency, and 64 is the age that my father retired. Similarly, to remember my ATM code 8374 (of course, now that I've told you my secret code, I'll need to memorize a new one!), I initially associated the chunk 83 with the age at which my grandmother passed away and 74 with the year my cousin Mike was born. Eventually, the numbers became so hardwired into my memory that the code now comes to me automatically and I don't need to use the association technique every time I go to the ATM. By applying the technique of associating meaningful facts with numbers, I find that I can remember even longer strings of numbers. For longer numbers, I simply lengthen each chunk to three or even four numbers. Note that creating meaningful associations with chunks can be somewhat of a challenge at first. However, many of my patients have found that exerting the extra effort to apply the chunking technique to commit something to memory pays off later when the time comes for them to recall it.

THE SIXTY-MINUTE BRAIN WORKOUT

Now it's time to put all of these memory improvement techniques into practice. Dr. George Rebok of the Johns Hopkins

University and I developed the Sixty-Minute Brain Workout especially for this book. As you may recall from our previous discussion on the effect of mental activity on the risk for Alzheimer's disease, Dr. Rebok is also the developer of the memory workout program of the much-publicized ACTIVE trial, the largest cognitive training experiment in the United States and sponsored by the National Institutes of Health (NIH). This trial proved that regular mental training can improve memory, concentration, and problem-solving skills even in people over the age of sixty-five. Just as in the Memory Stress Test, each of the exercises targets a specific cognitive domain and can be used for spot-training specific areas of brain weakness. I encourage you to refer back to your performance in the Memory Stress Test to see if you need to concentrate your efforts in a particular cognitive domain or if a general mental workout is all you need. Do not feel discouraged if initially you don't do as well as you think you should. Unlike the Memory Stress Test, keeping score here is not essential. These exercises are meant to push your mental abilities to the edge; you are not expected to have a perfect performance. To get the most of the brain workout, take time out of your busy schedule to exercise your mind at least two or three times a month. To avoid mental fatigue, I advise you to limit each exercise session to a maximum of sixty minutes. Make sure to apply the memory improvement techniques we talked about in this chapter and see how much easier it will be to perform these exercises. If any of these exercises causes you concern about your mental abilities, speak to your physician about whether a more thorough neuropsychological evaluation is appropriate.

EXERCISE 1: ATTENTION
AND CONCENTRATION

CONCENTRATION PRACTICE

Instructions:　Pick up a magazine from the newsstand or a book from the local library with plenty of pictures. Choose a busy picture and study it for a few minutes. Concentrate on as many details in the picture as you can. When you are finished looking at it, put it aside and write down as many details as you can remember. Now look at it again and attend to the things you have missed. Try writing down those details after studying the picture a few minutes.

CONCENTRATION PRACTICE

Instructions:　I don't typically recommend watching television as a way to improve your memory skills. However, the next time you watch one of your favorite shows, try doing the following: Before you turn on the TV or watch a movie, make a list of ten questions that will test your powers of concentration. For example, what are the names of the main characters in the show? What are the names of the actors and actresses who played those characters? What types of clothing were the different characters in the show wearing? How many different locations or settings were shown? At what times of day did the main actions occur? What types of furniture were used in the indoor scenes? Then, after the show ends, take out a blank sheet of paper and try to answer each of the questions on your list. Practice alone and with a friend. See if the two of you can remember more information than when you practiced alone.

CONCENTRATION PRACTICE

Instructions: Think about what your husband, wife, friend, neighbor, or co-worker wore this morning. Write down each person's name and the article of clothing he or she had on. Try to describe the clothing in as much detail as possible. At the end of the day, cover up the clothing descriptions and read each name. Then try to recall the clothing items associated with each person.

CONCENTRATION PRACTICE

Instructions: Answer the following questions to test how observant you are.

1. Which direction does Lincoln face on a penny—right or left?
2. What letters are missing from the telephone dial?
3. What color is at the top of the stoplight?
4. Which direction does water run down the drain?
5. Can you distinguish between a nickel and a dime by touch and without looking at them?

If you had difficulty answering these questions, try to focus more on the different features of things, using all of your senses. For example, try to recall a pet from childhood—say, a puppy. Do you remember its color, the softness of its fur, the sound of its bark, the feel of its tongue?

EXERCISE 2: LANGUAGE

STORY RECALL

Instructions: Have someone read the following story to you. Make sure the story is read in a clear, loud voice, pausing between sentences. When the person is done reading, try telling the story in your own words, but remember to mention as many of the main points and details as you can.

> *Josephine Davis, a kindergarten student, shocked spectators with a perfect performance of Beethoven's Fifth Symphony last night. She was inspired by a piano at Garden Place Mall. Mallgoers were astounded by the beautiful music. Said one mother, "I was just amazed that a little girl like that could play so well. The piano just seemed to take her over."*

Note: This story recall practice can be modified by substituting different information for the main idea units in the story: Jessica Flynn for Josephine Davis, Park View Plaza for Garden Place Mall, Gershwin's *Rhapsody in Blue* for Beethoven's Fifth Symphony, and so on.

LANGUAGE PRACTICE

Instructions: Read an article out of a current newspaper or magazine and tell a friend about it in your own words. Begin with a simple article on a topic that is familiar to you. If you are successful in doing this, try reading longer articles that deal with topics about which you know less. Ask your friend to check the article to see if you have omitted any important information.

EXERCISE 3: MEMORY

MEMORY FOR NAMES

Instructions: When you say good-bye to someone, try to make it a habit to repeat their name *("It was nice meeting you, Jim")*. Try to recall the name and face a short time later, and do this exercise for a few hours over the next few days.

MEMORY PRACTICE FOR NAMES AND FACES

Instructions: Cut out a dozen photographs of unfamiliar faces from a magazine or newspaper, give each person any name you like, and commit these names to your memory. Now try matching the name with each of the faces. Start off with three faces and then gradually work up to five or six. Try making the task more difficult by coming back to the photographs after an hour or so. If this proves too easy, come back to this task after a day or two to see how many of the names you still remember.

MEMORY PRACTICE FOR LISTS AND PHONE NUMBERS

Instructions: Have someone give you a list of ten items, such as a shopping list. Set your timer for a thirty-minute break and do something else that will distract you from the word list—watch TV, read the newspaper, what have you. After the thirty minutes, write down or recite as many items on the list as you can remember. You could try a similar exercise using phone numbers, trying to remember a number after a brief distraction. Have someone give you a phone number, occupy yourself for about a minute, and then try to recall the number.

MEMORY FOR INTENTIONS

Instructions: Have you ever entered a room in your house and forgotten why you went there in the first place? This experience is caused by a failure in your *memory for intention*—that is, remembering to do something that you intend to do at some future time. This exercise involves memory for intentions. You will be asked to do a task after you finish two memory exercises but before you do the third exercise. The exercises will involve memory for digits, words, and facts. Right after you complete the first two exercises (but not before), remember to write down the following four things on a pad of paper:

1. Your complete address
2. Your home phone number
3. Your birth date
4. The full name of your closest friend

Do not write this information down now and do not look back in this section to remind yourself. Now proceed to the first exercise.

Number List Forward

Instructions:　Have someone read each set of numbers to you aloud, pausing one second between each digit. Repeat the numbers in the *correct* order (For example, when a person reads the numbers "six four," you say, "six four"):

6-7
2-9-7
4-2-9-3
8-9-3-6-4
2-8-1-7-6-5
8-1-7-2-4-6-5
6-3-9-8-2-5-1-4

Word Recall

Instructions:　Have someone read you the following list of unrelated words, allowing for a one-second pause in between words. Then try to recall as many words as you can from the list. They do not have to be in any particular order. Take note of the number of words that you recalled correctly.

Bracelet
Hammer
Violet
Truck
Jelly
Dairy
Chin
Atlas
Teapot
Clarinet

MEMORY FOR FACTS

Instructions: Have someone read you the following list of names of the world's largest cities. See if you can memorize them in the order in which they are read, beginning with the largest city, Bombay.

1. Bombay
2. Buenos Aires
3. Seoul
4. Jakarta
5. Karachi
6. Manila
7. Sao Paulo

Did You Remember?

Did you remember to write out the information about yourself on a pad of paper before beginning the memory for facts exercise involving the names of the world's largest cities? If not, try to do it now without going back to read the instructions at the beginning of the exercise. Another way to practice your memory for intentions is given below.

MEMORY PRACTICE FOR INTENTIONS

Instructions: Write down a list of three things to do—make a phone call, reorganize the bookshelf, take out the garbage, or the like. Set your timer for a sixty-minute break and do something else that will distract you, such as watching TV or reading the newspaper. After the sixty minutes, try to remember all the things in your list. If this exercise proves too easy, try it again with a longer list and increase the amount of time (six hours, twenty-four hours, and so on) before you have to do something. Leave out the timer but have someone remind you in case you forget.

EXERCISE 4: EXECUTIVE FUNCTION

Go–No Go Task

Instructions: Have someone tap the bottom of a table two times. When they do, you tap the top of the table once. Then have them tap the bottom of the table once and you tap twice. If they tap the table three times, you should *not* tap at all. Have the person randomly alternate among tapping once, twice, or three times, and you respond by tapping twice, once, or not at all.

Pattern Recognition 1

Instructions: Read the list of months below. As you read the list out loud, see if you can begin to see a pattern developing. At the end of the list, say the name of the month that would come next in the list and follow the pattern.

January
January
February
March
March
April
May
May

PATTERN RECOGNITION 2

Instructions: Read the list of days below. As you read the list out loud, see if you can begin to see a pattern developing. At the end of the list, say the name of the day that would come next in the list and follow the pattern.

Saturday
Sunday
Monday
Monday
Tuesday
Wednesday
Thursday
Thursday
Friday
Saturday
Sunday

PATTERN RECOGNITION 3

Instructions: Read the lists of letters below. As you read each list out loud, try to see a pattern developing. At the end of each list, say the name of the letter that would come next in the list and follow the pattern.

J J K L L M N N ___
A B A B C D C D E F E F G H G H ___
T O P A B T O P C D T O P E F T O P G H ___

End of Workout

PRACTICE TIPS TO HELP YOU REMEMBER

ATTENTION

1. Alter your physical environment to make it easier to concentrate: *Remove distracting clutter and pictures in the work space. Replace fancy computer screensavers with simpler ones.*
2. Simplify work flow such that only one task, instead of multiple simultaneous tasks, is performed at a time: *Turn the television or radio off while paying the bills. Turn the cell phone off before getting into the driver's seat of the car.*
3. Give yourself tangible rewards for sustained work: *Take a coffee break or a short walk outside on a nice day after every couple of hours of continuous work.*

LANGUAGE

1. Turn to the crossword puzzle section of the morning paper and spend a few minutes every morning doing some mental calisthenics.
2. Pick up a new book and sharpen your comprehension of new stories and innovative concepts.
3. Learn to love new words by looking up their meanings and consciously making them part of your vocabulary.

MEMORY

1. Utilize visual imagery to remember new names or appointments—for instance, picture a tree growing in the middle of the waiting area of your doctor's office to remember a 3 P.M. doctor's appointment.

2. Habitually put your keys, glasses, and other things you tend to lose in only one place to minimize the chance of losing them.

3. Whenever possible, use an external memory aid to help you remember things that you want or need to do:

   Record appointments or things-to-do in your date book or on your wall calendar.

   Get into the habit of looking at your calendar twice a day and at bedtime.

   Change the location of a piece of furniture in a room to trigger the intention (for example, turn the kitchen chair or microwave around to remind yourself to take a medication at lunchtime).

   Ask a friend to remind you of the intention.

   Use a voice recorder if it is convenient to record your intention.

CALCULATION

1. Figure out the correct change or the right tip in your mind every time you have the opportunity.

2. Dig up your children's old math books and brush up on your algebra and word problems skills.

3. Balance your checkbook using only a pen and paper before confirming its accuracy with a calculator.

EXECUTIVE FUNCTION

1. Organize tasks that require multiple steps in your mind before performing them; for more complicated tasks, write the individual steps down and follow them as you would a cookbook.

2. Try your hand at some jigsaw puzzles to improve your visual and motor skills.
3. File things according to a logical sequence to avoid confusion at a future time.

THE ROAD TO AN AGE-PROOF MIND

In this chapter, I introduced you to some powerful memory improvement techniques, mental exercises to strengthen your mind, and practical tips to help you remember better. Now that you are equipped with the necessary knowledge and tools for keeping your mind as healthy and sharp for as long as possible, it is time to incorporate all this information into your daily life. In the next chapter, I will condense and summarize the information I have presented in the last twelve chapters into ten simple steps to an age-proof mind. Following these steps can tip the odds of a robust memory and intellectual function decidedly in your mind's favor.

Chapter 13

Age-Proof Your Mind

"The best memory is that which forgets nothing but injuries.
Write kindness in marble and write injuries in the dust."

—PERSIAN PROVERB

How would you define a successfully lived life? Would you judge it by its high degree of health and exceptional longevity? Or perhaps by the wealth of wisdom and life satisfaction achieved by the individual? In medicine, cognitive success is measured by people's ability to maintain a level of mental ability that allows them to interact effectively and appropriately with the environment and the other people who live in it. The specific levels of mental abilities that are necessary to be considered "successful" are as varied as the lifestyles that people choose to lead. For some it may only require the performance of basic abilities to solve the simple problems of daily life, such as when to take a medication or how to operate a microwave. For others, more complicated mental abilities are required, such as analyzing a strategic business plan in a company board meeting or tutoring a grandchild on how to solve a difficult mathematical problem. In other words, successful brain aging is simply a state where your mental abilities do not interfere with your chosen way of life. This implies that it is not possible to use a single, universal yardstick to measure successful brain aging. Instead, the measure of success of cognitive status should be tailored according to a person's particular life situation.

Other brain experts may not necessarily agree with my practical view on this matter. Some define successful brain aging more rigidly, such as memory test scores that place people in the upper strata for their age and educational background.[1] This criterion, while easier to measure and perhaps more valid for research purposes, is inherently biased against people who never possessed superior intelligence even during their youth. Baseline intelligence, unlike age and educational attainment, cannot be easily measured. Other important factors such as cultural and language differences are also difficult, if not impossible, to standardize. For these reasons, I believe that successful brain aging is best measured by the capacity of a person's mind to maintain optimal physical, social, and psychological health, rather than by memory test scores alone.

SUCCESSFUL AGING IN AMERICA: THE MacARTHUR FOUNDATION STUDY

The MacArthur Foundation Network on Successful Aging is an interdisciplinary collaboration of researchers all over the United States who came together in 1984 to define successful

---

1. Albert MS, Jones K, Savage CR, Berkman L, Seeman T, Blazer D. Predictors of cognitive change in older persons: MacArthur Studies of Successful Aging. *Psych Aging* 1995;10:578–589.

aging, American style. More than four thousand people living across the United States and ranging in age from seventy to seventy-nine years were studied for this purpose.[2] After performing physical and mental examinations, the researchers identified a subgroup of 1,192 individuals who enjoyed good or excellent psychological and physical health. These "high-functioning" people were then compared with others of similar age who had significant mental and physical disabilities.

The MacArthur Study researchers found that while *biological* factors were the most powerful forces that controlled growth and development during early life, *lifestyle* factors became a more potent force in maintaining health as people age. In other words, the older we get, the greater the impact of the environment on our health. Compared to "usually" aging people, successfully aging people had better diets, smoked fewer cigarettes, exercised more, had better lung function, and tended to rate their health much higher. The researchers further found that successfully aging people had higher levels of educational attainment. This reinforced the connection between intellectual stimulation and mental health as previously reported by the Nun Study.

One of the most interesting findings of the MacArthur Study is the vital role of a person's emotional state in maintaining intellectual abilities in later life. *Self-efficacy* is defined as the belief that through your actions, you can produce a desired effect. It is the perception that you have control over your immediate environment. Successfully aging people have

2. Berkman LF, Seeman TE, Albert M, et al. High, usual and impaired functioning in community-dwelling older men and women: findings from the MacArthur Foundation Research Network on Successful Aging. *J Clin Epidemiol* 1993;46:1129–1140.

high scores in ratings of self-efficacy, convinced that they have control over their health and the power to alter its course. Compared to modern- and low-functioning older people, they are also less likely to be anxious or depressed. Self-efficacious people are more psychologically stable, have less pronounced age-related declines in intellectual abilities, and enjoy better general health status.

The MacArthur Study has shown that your genes can only take you so far in life. The rest of the way, you need to positively modify your internal and external environment in order to reach the goal of successful aging. In the following section, I will outline the steps you should be taking now to help your mind age slowly and gracefully.

TEN STEPS TO AN AGE-PROOF MIND

The road to successful brain aging is a path that is not very well traveled. Most people are still at a loss when navigating the treacherous waters of mental aging. Fortunately, good scientific evidence has provided us with valuable signposts that point us in the right direction. I have interpreted and condensed into ten simple steps the multitude of research studies on how to dodge the nefarious effects of age and disease on brain health. They are the same set of advice that I give to patients who come to my clinic for memory problems and leave with the hope that they can do something about it.

Your mind is unique in the entire universe; no one else could possibly have shared your exact experiences and kept identical memories. Thus, a cookie-cutter approach to the promotion of brain health runs counter to everything that we have talked about so far. Discuss these steps with your doctor to see which ones are right for you. Because certain factors such as genes and childhood environmental exposures can no longer be altered, following these steps may not prevent Alzheimer's disease in everyone. However, the state of the science on successful brain aging supports the value of these interventions in tipping the odds in your mind's favor.

Step 1. Challenge Your Mind

The detrimental effects of intellectual stagnation on the mind are well supported by numerous scientific studies. The Nun Study and the MacArthur Study have shown the protective effect of education on the development of Alzheimer's disease and premature intellectual decline. The act of going to school itself cannot explain the mind-preserving effects of education. More likely, the habits of lifelong learning and techniques of analytical thinking fostered by education are the ones responsible for this. It is never too late to challenge your mind. Learning and intellectual stimulation at any age can alter the physical and functional characteristics of your brain, imparting it with a greater degree of plasticity. The more plastic brain has a greater functional reserve, which offers a protective buffer against the ravages of time and disease. Regular mental calisthenics are one good way to challenge the mind and build reserves. They have been shown to be effective in maintaining a good memory in healthy adults even during their later years. *The Memory Workout Program provided in this book is a great way to jump-start your mind.*

Step 2. Get Physically Fit and Active

The health of the heart and the brain are closely intertwined. Lifestyle interventions, including regular exercise and a healthy diet, which were once thought to be beneficial only to the heart, have been shown to be good for the brain as well. Regular physical activity promotes good cardiovascular and lung health, characteristics shared by people whose minds are also successfully aging. Exercise wards off depression and promotes a good sense of general well-being that can optimize intellectual abilities. There are many enjoyable forms of physical activity suited for different life situations and physical limitations. *The best types of activity are those that are both physically and mentally challenging, such as dancing or learning a new sport.* Make sure to consult your doctor before starting a physical activity program.

Step 3. Think Before You Eat

Scientific studies are continuing to forge the links between diet and the aging mind. A diet that is low in calories and saturated fats and high in antioxidants and polyunsaturated fatty acids (PUFA) has a good chance of lowering your risk for Alzheimer's. High caloric intake leads to the generation of harmful oxygen free radicals that can damage the brain's memory cells. A diet rich in antioxidants or the intake of antioxidant vitamin supplements may neutralize these toxic forms of oxygen.

The following are general nutritional guidelines to help you achieve an age-proof mind:

1. Healthy, moderately active adults should aim for a daily caloric intake between eighteen and twenty-two hundred calories.
2. Antioxidant-rich foods such as blueberries, broccoli, carrots, kale, soybeans, and grapes should be incorporated in the diet whenever possible.
3. Substitute a serving of fish packed with beneficial omega-3 fatty acids for meats and dairy products at least once or twice a week.
4. People who are unable to modify their diet and those at high risk for Alzheimer's disease based on family history should discuss with their physicians whether taking 400 to 800 IU per day of vitamin E supplements is advisable.
5. Take a multivitamin daily. Other vitamins and minerals are also important for optimal brain health. Deficiencies in vitamin B and carotenoids have been linked to memory problems, while zinc and vitamin D are required for normal nerve function. Further, a harmful rise in homocysteine levels occurs when the diet is deficient in folic acid and vitamins B_{12} and B_6.

Step 4. Be Vigilant of Your Mind's Abilities

We are at the dawn of an era in brain research that promises to match the advances achieved for cardiovascular disease in the past century. Brain scientists are at the cusp of discovering effective interventions that will prevent the progression of MCI to Alzheimer's disease. More than ever, it is important for you to be aware of your mind's strengths and weaknesses. This is the only way that you will recognize the appearance of the earliest signs of a memory problem. *Keep track of your perfor-mance on the Memory Stress Test and consult your physician if you feel that your abilities have declined to a significant degree.* A more comprehensive neuropsychological test may be neces-sary to determine the state of your mind's health. Be more aware as well of a spouse's or parent's present mental status, even if you think that your loved ones are completely normal. The time may come when the judgment on the health of their memory will hinge on your accurate and objective assessment of their past abilities. If you suspect a problem in a loved one's memory, begin describing episodes of forgetfulness in a mem-ory diary to keep track of the frequency, severity, and rate of progression of the problem.

Step 5. Learn and Apply Memory Improvement Techniques

At the peak of our careers, many of us push the finite limits of our memory and attention by taking on several tasks at the same time. As our lives become more complicated, we become more dependent on memory crutches to help us keep track of the many balls we have in the air. But as we approach the age of retirement, our memory and other mental abilities have a tendency to become less efficient even as our lives become simpler. It is at this stage of our lives that we could use the help of memory techniques to help us through certain humps. This is where the memory improvement strategies come in. *Visualization, association, method of loci, and chunking are just some of the strategies this book has discussed. Begin practicing these techniques now. They were designed to enhance learning and the efficiency of the aging mind.*

Step 6. Search Your Gene Pool for Memory Problems

People with first-degree relatives afflicted with Alzheimer's disease are at an increased risk of getting memory problems themselves. Trace your family tree to discover any genetic predisposition to degenerative brain diseases. Of note, simply inquiring about a diagnosis of Alzheimer's disease is moot since forgetfulness occurring in older people was not formally given this label in the past. Instead, ask the older members of your family if any of your relatives became forgetful during their later years. They may have been falsely given a diagnosis of senility or hardening of the arteries. *Get as much information on your family history as you can and see if the pattern of forgetfulness matches that of Alzheimer's disease as described in earlier chapters of this book.* People with a strong family history of memory problems should be especially wary of the health of their mind and speak to their physicians about possible preventive interventions (see the next step).

Step 7. Speak to Your Doctor About Statins, Ibuprofen, and Homocysteine

People who have a strong family history of Alzheimer's disease stand to benefit the most from interventions aimed at combating premature brain degeneration. *The anti-inflammatory medication ibuprofen and the cholesterol-lowering medications statins have been associated with a lower incidence of Alzheimer's in people who took them regularly. Antioxidants such as vitamin E may even slow down the aging of the mind.* Large clinical trials are testing the long-term efficacy and safety of these medicines in preventing the disease in people who have normal memory abilities. While it would be premature to recommend these medications for prevention of memory problems, I would advise people who are at high risk of getting Alzheimer's to at least speak to their physicians about them. *People with a family history of premature coronary artery disease and/or dementia should also consider having their serum homocysteine levels checked.* If their homocysteine levels are high, taking therapeutic doses of folic acid and vitamins B_6 and B_{12} under the guidance of their doctors will be an appropriate intervention. Finally, people who live in certain metropolitan areas should look into the possibility of participating in research trials of medications for the primary prevention of Alzheimer's disease. Refer to the Resources section at the end of this book to find out where you can go to obtain more information on ongoing clinical trials in your area.

Step 8. Kill Stress

Stress is an environmental factor that becomes more detrimental to mental and physical health as we age. The brain's perception of a threat triggers a series of hormonal and nervous reactions whose aim is to neutralize the stressor through the classic fight-or-flight response. The stress reaction is meant only to be a brief, lifesaving defense mechanism. When allowed to persist over longer periods of time, it becomes a maladaptive response that ultimately leads to harm. For years, we have known that a stressful lifestyle is one of the risk factors for a heart attack. More recent research has shown that sustained stress levels are also damaging to the brain. The brain reacts to physical or psychological stress by inducing the adrenal gland (a pair of small glands adjacent to the kidneys) to produce the stress hormone *cortisol*. Cortisol is a form of steroid that can alter the body's metabolism by increasing blood sugar, breaking down proteins, and releasing fats from storage. The overall effect of these changes is a rapid rise in available energy that the individual can use to deal with the stressor. However, sustained elevations of cortisol produce many adverse effects throughout the body and to the brain.[3] The nefarious effect of cortisol on memory has been the subject of numerous research studies. For instance, healthy volunteers who were exposed to a brief psychological stress experienced a rise in their cortisol levels and a corresponding decline in their memory performance.[4] Similarly, the administration of 10 mg of cortisol to volunteers caused memory impairment even when they did not experience stress. The bad effects of stress have also been observed in real-life settings. A study showed that women with jobs that place them in situations of high demand, low control, and low social support experienced the greatest decline in intellectual and physical functioning over time.[5]

In the competitive and fast-paced world that we live in, it is virtually impossible to completely avoid stress. However, the scientific evidence points to the importance of dodging unnecessary and sustained stress. *In the interest of successful brain aging, we must try to keep our life stressors to a bare minimum.*

---

3. Liu J, Mori A. Stress, aging and brain oxidative damage. *Neurochem Res* 1999;24:11479–11497.
4. Kirschbaum C, Wolf OT, May M, et al. Stress and treatment-induced elevations of cortisol levels associated with impaired declarative memory in healthy adults. *Life Sci* 1996;58: 1475–1483.
5. Cheng Y, Kawachi I, Coakley EH, et al. Association between psychological work characteristics and health functioning in American women: prospective study. *Brit Med J* 2000;320: 1432–1483.

Step 9. Seek Treatment for Depression

Depression is a medical condition characterized by a constant feeling of sadness, lack of energy, and inability to concentrate. It can cause the person to become irritable and lose interest or pleasure in usual activities and hobbies. Some people have described depression as a black curtain of despair coming down on their lives. Distinct from the psychological state of sadness, it is caused by an imbalance of chemicals in the brain. Depression requires medical treatment to bring back the state of balance.

People suffering from depression may sometimes be mistaken for those suffering from a memory problem. But their poor mental performance is primarily due to their inability to concentrate and their loss of interest in life, rather than to a primary problem with memory. When depression is allowed to persist for a long time, however, it may directly affect memory and even lead to dementia. Like chronic stress, depression has been shown to cause a rise in cortisol levels in the bloodstream. Along with this comes the associated pernicious effect of a sustained elevation of cortisol on the brain. Magnetic resonance imaging (MRI) studies performed on people suffering from depression showed a decrease in size of several brain areas, including the short-term memory center in the hippocampus.[6] This suggests that the high cortisol levels may induce brain degeneration, which may ultimately result in memory impairment. The selective serotonin reuptake inhibitors (SSRIs) are the most widely used group of medicines

6. Sheline YI, Sangavi M, Mintum MA, Gado MH. Depression duration but not age predicts hippocampal volume loss in medically healthy women with recurrent major depression. *J Neurosci* 1999;19:5034–5043.

to treat this condition. These are more popularly known in the United States by such brand names as Zoloft, Prozac, Paxil, and Celexa. Interestingly, the SSRI class of medications has been shown to stimulate brain cell regeneration within the hippocampus.[7]

If you feel that you may have depression, it is important to discuss this with your physician. Many effective and safe medicines, as well as nonpharmacologic interventions such as psychotherapy and support groups, are available. *Nipping depression in the bud is an essential step toward age-proofing your mind.*

Step 10. Take Control of Your Mind

Many of my patients' children have confided to me the deep feeling of helplessness they experience when their own risk of succumbing to Alzheimer's disease crosses their mind. They feel helpless because they believe that nothing can be done to alter the fate of their minds. But the weight of scientific evidence does not support this belief. In this book, I have discussed ways to identify and reduce your risk of becoming a victim of degenerative brain conditions such as Alzheimer's disease. The wise reader will do well to keep these in mind. While a healthy awareness of the state of your memory is good, needlessly worrying about it is not. *People who are overly concerned about their memory should forget about forgetting and focus instead on how to remember better.* The MacArthur Study on successful aging proved that people who feel in control of

7. Duman RS, Malberg J, Nakagawa S, D'Sa C. Neuronal plasticity and survival in mood disorders. *Biological Psychiatry* 2000;48:732–739.

their lives are less likely to experience memory problems. Those who consider themselves helpless victims of fate have a greater chance of becoming forgetful later in life. It is therefore imperative for all of us to remember that the destiny of our minds is within our control.

STEPPING INTO THE FUTURE

The preceding ten steps to an age-proof mind represent the state of the science in the prevention of age-related decline in memory and other intellectual functions. The sooner you start these steps, the more likely they are to make a positive difference in the future of your mind. As you begin to alter the way you live for the betterment of your intellectual health, you should also be aware of the brightest prospects for battling diseases that can cause your memory to decline. In the next chapter, I will give you a sneak peek at what's on the horizon for preventing, treating, and curing Alzheimer's disease. Learn about these prospects now to know what you can expect in the near future.

Chapter 14

The Future Promise of an Alzheimer's Cure

"Forty is the old age of youth, fifty is the youth of old age."
—VICTOR HUGO

In the United States alone, more than four million people are currently afflicted with Alzheimer's disease. Approximately 10 percent of people over the age of sixty-five and 50 percent of those over eighty-five have the disease. Alzheimer's touches the lives of countless other people around them, and their numbers are growing exponentially. As you read this book, the ravages of time and disease may be taking their toll on the precious brain cells where your memories are kept. Unless a cure is found soon, the rapidly aging baby boomer generation will cause the number of people in the United States with Alzheimer's disease to swell to fourteen million by the year 2050. The staggering numbers of people at risk for Alzheimer's disease is a ticking time bomb that can overwhelm our present systems of welfare and health care. It depletes the individual's sense of self and robs society of accumulated expertise and wisdom.

In a way, we truly are the victims of our own success. In ancient Rome, the average life expectancy was twenty-two years of age, and an average person born in the United States in 1900 was expected to live to a ripe old age of forty-nine years. In contrast, a person born in the year 2000 has an average life expectancy of seventy-seven years or longer. This is a testament to our society's triumphant success in curbing the number of deaths from war, infectious disease, and, more recently, heart disease. As scientific advances in medicine and public health continue by leaps and bounds, *life expectancy* is predicted to soon approach the biological upper limit of the human *life span* of 120 years. Ironically, the more successful we become at preventing and treating diseases such as heart disease and cancer, the more susceptible we become to Alzheimer's disease. This is why it is important for all of us to be more aware of our mind's health and what we can do now to keep it that way.

In this chapter, I will introduce you to the most promising ways to prevent, treat, and cure Alzheimer's disease. Some of the interventions I will be presenting here are still in the realm of research and clinical trials and may not yet be available in your doctor's office or pharmacy. Nonetheless, you should know about them now because these experimental interventions are likely to become the standard treatments in the near future. More information about these options and other cutting-edge research on Alzheimer's disease can be found at the Web site http://www.clinicaltrials.gov. There you can obtain additional information on how to participate in ongoing and future clinical trials for various diseases.

CURRENTLY AVAILABLE TREATMENT FOR ALZHEIMER'S DISEASE

The overarching goal of modern medicine is to prevent all diseases that contribute to premature death or disability. Because this is not possible, science has produced effective treatments for many diseases such as cancer, diabetes, stroke, and even the common cold for which there are still no cures. Like these conditions, Alzheimer's is a *treatable* but not a *curable* disease—not yet, anyway. All available treatments for this disease fall under one of two categories. *Symptomatic treatments* are those that alleviate some of the bothersome manifestations of the disease but do not treat its cause. In contrast, *disease–modifying treatments* can change the course of the disease by disrupting or counteracting the progress of its underlying cause. Most of the current U.S. Food and Drug Administration (FDA)–approved prescription medicines for Alzheimer's disease are symptomatic treatments that are designed primarily to improve the memory symptoms. The two most promising and widely used types of medication are donepezil (Aricept) and other acetylcholinesterase inhibitors, and memantine.

Aricept and Other Acetylcholinesterase Inhibitors

For many years, the class of medications called *acetylcholinesterase inhibitors* was the only available medicine for Alzheimer's disease. These medicines can alleviate some of the most disabling symptoms of the disease by improving memory and functional ability. Included under this class of medications are donepezil, rivastigmine, and galantamine, perhaps better known by their trade names Aricept, Exelon, and Reminyl, respectively. Acetylcholinesterase inhibitors act directly on brain cells by preventing the breakdown of the substance called *acetylcholine*, the chemical used by nerve cells to communicate with each other. Acetylcholine has been shown to be abnormally low in people with Alzheimer's disease. By inhibiting its destruction by enzymes, these medications can increase acetylcholine concentrations, improve the flow of communication among brain cells, and facilitate information transfer. Clinical trials have shown that these medications have beneficial effects on memory and other mental functions when given to people with mild to moderate Alzheimer's disease. Of note, there is not enough evidence to support their use in the late stages of the disease. However, there is some evidence that acetylcholinesterase inhibitors may treat the behavioral symptoms associated with dementia and perhaps even delay the progression of the underlying disease. If this is proven to be true by future studies, these medications become potentially useful treatments even for people with advanced disease.

People who are given a prescription for an acetylcholinesterase inhibitor by their physician must understand that it does not cause an improvement in memory in everyone. Further, taking this medication is *not* likely to cure their disease. Those who do derive benefit from it typically experience only modest improvements in memory and function. The degree of improvement is not dramatic: At best the medication will return the patient to a level of function equivalent to that of six to twelve months prior to starting the medication. It cannot reverse the hands of time and give back a completely normal memory. Acetylcholinesterase inhibitors are usually well tolerated, but side effects such as nausea, vomiting, and diarrhea may occur.

Memantine

In late 2003, the FDA gave its all-important seal of approval to the new drug memantine. In contrast to the acetylcholinesterase inhibitors, which are FDA-approved only for mild to moderate dementia, memantine is approved for the treatment of people with moderate to severe dementia. It became available on U.S. pharmacy shelves in 2004, sparking a glimmer of hope in people with advanced stages of Alzheimer's disease, for which there was no previously available treatment. Far from being a novel treatment, memantine has been available in Germany for the treatment of various neurological illnesses for more than ten years. One thing that makes this drug attractive is its unique mechanism of action, which is entirely different from that of acetylcholinesterase inhibitors. This characteristic opened the possibility for the use of memantine as a supplemental or combination therapy along with Aricept and similar drugs.

Memantine works by controlling the activity of *glutamate*, another brain messenger chemical involved with the processing, storage, and retrieval of information. Glutamate triggers a brain receptor called N-methyl-D-aspartate (NMDA), which in turn allows minute amounts of calcium to flow into the nerve cells. This is the process that makes memory and learning possible. But in Alzheimer's disease, glutamate *overstimulates* the NMDA receptors, allowing too much calcium to get into the brain cell. The abnormally high concentrations of calcium eventually kill the cells. Memantine protects the brain cells by blocking the NMDA receptors from stimulation by glutamate.

To find out if memantine really works, researchers studied 252 people from thirty-two centers around the United States who had moderate to severe Alzheimer's disease. The participants received either 20 mg of memantine (10 mg twice a day) or placebo pills daily. After seven months, the researchers found that the people who took memantine suffered less deterioration in their memory and in their ability to perform their activities of daily living compared to those who only received placebo pills. Moreover, the drug was surprisingly well tolerated, without any significant side effects. Memantine can also be used as an add-on treatment. A study found that at a dose of 10 mg twice a day, memantine caused an improvement in the memory, behavior, and functional abilities of people with moderate or advanced Alzheimer's disease who were already taking donepezil.[1]

Although memantine is both effective and safe for moderate to severe Alzheimer's disease, it is unfortunately not the magic memory pill that we are all hoping for. It can neither permanently reverse memory loss nor cure the disease. But one thing that it has going for it is its potential to alter the course of Alzheimer's disease. Unlike Aricept and similar medications that are only symptomatic treatments for Alzheimer's, memantine is believed to be a disease-modifying treatment. This means that taking this medication on a long-term basis may actually decrease the rate of progression of the memory problems.

It will take several more years of clinical trials to determine whether memantine will hold up to this promise. We also do not know whether this medication is effective and safe for people in the early stages of a memory problem, including those with MCI or those with mild Alzheimer's disease. At present, only people with moderate to severe Alzheimer's are good

---

1. Tariot PN, Farlow MR, Grossberg GT, et al. Memantine treatment in patients with moderate to severe Alzheimer's disease already receiving donepezil. *J Am Med Assoc* 2004;291:317–324.

candidates for treatment with memantine either as single therapy or in combination with an acetylcholinesterase inhibitor.

THE ALZHEIMER'S VACCINE

The height of optimism for finding the elusive Alzheimer's disease cure was reached in the year 2000. The Dublin-based company Elan Pharmaceuticals proclaimed that it had found a way to dissolve the abnormal amyloid plaques long suspected as the culprit in the brain cell death and forgetfulness of Alzheimer's disease. The vaccine code-named AN-1792 was composed of the very same protein that gave rise to the nefarious brain plaques. When it was injected into mutant mice that had been genetically programmed to develop Alzheimer's disease, their immune systems developed antibodies against the amyloid protein, sweeping their brains clean of the plaques. In fact, the brains of the vaccinated mice had up to 90 percent fewer plaques than mice that did not receive the vaccine.[2] Moreover, the vaccinated mice performed superbly in a water maze test designed to assess working memory, with scores comparable to those of normal mice.[3] These encouraging results opened the door to a clinical trial that tested whether the vaccine had a similar positive effect on humans.

An initial study of a hundred volunteers with mild to moderate Alzheimer's showed that the vaccine was safe. But when researchers expanded the study to include 360 people living in

2. Schenk D, Barbour R, Dunn W, et al. Immunization with amyloid-beta attenuates Alzheimer-disease-like pathology in the PDAPP mouse. *Nature* 1999;400(6740):173–177.
3. Morgan D, Diamond DM, Gottschall PE, et al. A beta peptide vaccination prevents memory loss in an animal model of Alzheimer's disease. *Nature* 2000;408(6815):982–985.

four European countries and eleven U.S. cities, early hope for the vaccine was given a crushing blow. Alas, what proved to be safe for mice was not found to be so in humans. Fifteen volunteers developed serious brain inflammation, in some cases leading to death. By March 2002, the vaccine's manufacturer announced that it was permanently abandoning the AN-1792 vaccine in favor of further research for a safer Alzheimer's cure. A later study showed that the brains of people who died from the vaccine trial were infiltrated with T cells, a type of white blood cell not normally found in the brain. The researchers hypothesized that the immune system may have overreacted to the vaccine, causing damage to normal brain tissue, inflammation, and abnormal brain swelling.

All hope for the Alzheimer's vaccine is not yet lost. Its manufacturers are working on reintroducing a reformulated form in the near future. But serious challenges are awaiting its arrival. After it is conclusively shown to be safe in humans, the manufacturers must still prove that the Alzheimer's vaccine is effective in reducing the amount of amyloid plaques and, more importantly, in improving the memory of people with Alzheimer's and preventing memory problems in people who are at risk of getting the disease. These are big hurdles that will take at least several years to overcome. Still, the promise of a vaccine preventing brain degeneration is something worth waiting for.

ALZHEIMER'S ENZYME BLOCKERS

Another promising approach to the disruption of the process that results in the accumulation of harmful amyloid plaques in the Alzheimer's brain is the blockage of a critical enzyme involved in their creation. Scientists from several pharmaceutical companies and research laboratories are hard at work in search of ways to block these enzymes. But before such an enzyme-blocking drug can be developed and tested in humans, scientists are first making sure that the enzymes do not play other roles in vital metabolic functions elsewhere in the body. If they do, drugs that block their action may harm another organ even as it protects the brain from Alzheimer's disease. Many more years of research will be required before these important issues are resolved. If researchers are successful in developing a safe and effective enzyme inhibitor in the future, the treatment of Alzheimer's may become very similar to that of diabetes, where taking a pill or an injection daily will effectively control the disease.

NERVE GROWTH STIMULATORS

Developing nerve cells produce substances called *growth factors* during the process of brain maturation. These growth factors play a crucial role in normal brain cell proliferation and differentiation. Cerebrolysin is a new drug that mimics the effects of naturally occurring growth factors and may stimulate the growth and development of new brain cells in people with Alzheimer's disease. In a clinical drug trial performed by Chinese investigators, intravenous infusions of cerebrolysin given to about 150 volunteers who had mild to moderate Alzheimer's disease five days a week caused measurable improvements in memory and other cognitive functions after only four weeks of treatment.[4] This is preliminary evidence of the drug's possible role in treatment of Alzheimer's. Larger clinical trials are ongoing to assess its safety and efficacy for this purpose and its possible utility for other neurological diseases such as strokes. Cerebrolysin is in the process of securing FDA approval and is not yet commercially available in the United States.

SELECTED CLINICAL PREVENTION TRIALS FOR ALZHEIMER'S DISEASE[5]

Alzheimer's Disease Anti-inflammatory Prevention Trial (ADAPT)

Inflammation is one of the primary mechanisms by which amyloid plaques are believed to cause Alzheimer's disease. The U.S. National Institute on Aging (NIA) is sponsoring a trial that will test the effectiveness and safety of the long-term use of the anti-inflammatory medications naproxen (Aleve) and celecoxib (Celexa) in the prevention of Alzheimer's disease and age-related cognitive decline. The study is being conducted in six U.S. cities: Baltimore, Boston, Phoenix, Seattle, Tampa, and Rochester, New York, and will involve about twenty-six hundred individuals. The study is slated to run for five to seven years. Further details can

---

4. Shifu X, Heqin Y, Peifen Y. Efficacy of FPF 1070 (cerebrolysin) in patients with Alzheimer's disease. *Clin Drug Invest* 2000;19(1):43–53.
5. This list is current as of September 2004; to get an updated list of ongoing clinical trials in your city, go to http://www.clinicaltrials.gov.

be found at the National Institutes of Health Web site: http://www.clinicaltrials.gov.

Prevention of Alzheimer's Disease by Vitamin E and Selenium (PREADVISE)

The generation of toxic oxygen free radicals is another major mechanism that has been implicated in Alzheimer's disease. An imbalance between the rate of oxygen radical formation and its deactivation by antioxidants is believed to result in brain cell damage and memory loss. The NIA is sponsoring a trial that will investigate the safety and effectiveness of the antioxidants vitamin E and selenium in preventing Alzheimer's disease. This seven- to ten-year trial is actually a part of a bigger study that is examining the ability of the two antioxidants to prevent prostate cancer. Thus, only men between the ages of sixty and ninety years are eligible to participate in this study. The participants will be given 400 IU of vitamin E and 200 mcg of selenium daily. More information on this study, including the eligibility criteria, can be found at the National Institutes of Health Web site: http://www.clinicaltrials.gov.

Preventing Cognitive Decline with Alternative Therapies

Complementary and alternative medicines (CAM) are proving to be a formidable force in the quest for a way to prevent Alzheimer's disease. Foremost among the many available CAM treatments for brain health is *Ginkgo biloba*. The National Center for Complementary and Alternative Medicine (NCCAM) is sponsoring a trial that will test ginkgo as a preventive measure against MCI and Alzheimer's disease in a group of two hundred volunteers. The study is limited to the most elderly (eighty-five years of age or more) because as a group, they are at the greatest risk of developing memory problems. More information about this trial is presented at the NCCAM Web site: http://nccam.nih.gov.

SELECTED CLINICAL TREATMENT TRIALS FOR ALZHEIMER'S DISEASE

Cholesterol Lowering Agents to Slow Progression of Alzheimer's Disease (CLASP)

The drugs known as statins are the most popular cholesterol-lowering agents in the United States. People know these medications better by their brand names Lipitor, Zocor, Lescol, and Pravachol through direct-to-consumer TV and print advertising by the pharmaceutical companies. While primarily used to treat elevated cholesterol levels and to reduce heart attacks, the use of statins has also been associated with a lowering of the risk for Alzheimer's disease. The mechanism by which statins do this is currently unknown, but may be related to the reduction of brain inflammation and oxidation.

The CLASP study sponsored by the National Institute on Aging will test the safety and efficacy of the statin drug simvastatin (Zocor) in treating people with mild to moderate Alzheimer's disease. To be eligible for this study, participants must satisfy a set of criteria outlined on the National

Institutes of Health's Web site (http://www.nih.gov). An ongoing manufacturer-sponsored trial is also testing the utility of another statin medication, atorvastatin (Lipitor), to treat people with mild Alzheimer's. These studies will shed light to the possible role of statins in the treatment of the disease. If cholesterol-lowering medications are shown to be effective and safe in delaying the progression of Alzheimer's disease, a primary prevention trial of these medications is sure to follow.

Ampalex (CX516)

Glutamate is a type of amino acid (building blocks of protein) that is used by certain types of brain cells to communicate with others. It does this by attaching to a docking or receptor site called *AMPA* (short for *alpha-amino-2,3-dihydro-5-methyl-3-oxo-4-isoxazolepropanoic acid*). In Alzheimer's disease, the brain cells that produce glutamate are damaged. Scientists believe that the stimulation of the AMPA receptor will facilitate communication among brain cells and possibly alleviate some of the symptoms of Alzheimer's disease. Ampalex (CX516) is a new drug that has the capability of exciting the AMPA receptors. The National Institute of Neurologic Disorders and Stroke (NINDS) is sponsoring a clinical trial that will test the safety and effectiveness of this drug in people with Alzheimer's disease. A small initial study of Ampalex shows that it is well tolerated and can enhance learning and memory in healthy young and elderly adults. More information about the trial can be found at the NINDS Web site: http://www.ninds.nih.gov.

CHANGE OF HEART, CHANGE OF MIND

Not too long ago, virtually everyone accepted heart disease as an inevitable aspect of growing old. In medical schools around the world, future physicians were taught that atherosclerosis (narrowing of the arteries from deposits of fat) naturally occurs as people age, and that blood pressure normally rises with age to allow the heart to pump blood through the narrowed arteries. At that time, many physicians did not believe that a person could prevent or reverse heart disease by regular exercise, lowering cholesterol, and avoiding certain environmental exposures such as tobacco. In fact, in the 1950s, advertising billboards depicting a fellow clad in a white coat enjoying a cigarette and slogans such as "More doctors smoke Camels than any other cigarette" and "L&M cigarettes: Just what the doctor ordered" were quite popular. Fifty years later, these have become mere relics of our not-so-distant, misinformed past. Now everyone knows that narrowed arteries can lead to heart attacks, and high blood pressure can precipitate a stroke. We have also learned that certain lifestyle and behavior modifications, such as staying away from cigarette smoke, are powerful ways of preventing heart disease. Our knowledge of and attitudes toward heart disease have indeed changed by leaps and bounds in just a few decades. How would you predict our views on the inevitability of Alzheimer's disease and age-associated memory loss would change in the next few decades?

By a proclamation from the president of the United States, the decade 1990–2000 was designated the Decade of the Brain. Millions of dollars of public funds were funneled into a concerted effort that accelerated neuroscience research and increased public awareness of diseases that can afflict the

mind. As a result, astounding progress was made in this period, shaping our current understanding of Alzheimer's as
well as other diseases. In this book, I have presented the latest
and most promising findings in the ongoing quest for the prevention and cure for age-related memory decline. I hope you
make use of this knowledge wisely by putting it into practice
in your daily life. Use the Memory Stress Test to assess and
keep track of your mental abilities. Allow the Sixty-Minute
Brain Workout program to regularly challenge and sharpen
your mind. And finally, follow the ten steps to an age-proof
mind and begin taking charge of the future of your mind
now—because tomorrow might be too late.

Appendix A

Food for Thought: Recipes for a Healthier Mind and Body

The following recipe suggestions have been prepared especially for this book by Ms. Sayaka Mitsuhashi[1] of the Okinawa Centenarian Study. They are packed with antioxidants and essential vitamins but are low in calories and saturated fats. Detailed nutritional information is provided at the end of each recipe.

[1] Saya_Mitsuhashi@nifty.com.

Peach Almond Smoothie

SERVES 4

This simple-to-prepare drink is packed with antioxidants, vita-mins, and minerals. It can be taken as a fresh start to the morning or to quickly ease hunger and satisfy a sweet craving. When using canned peaches, choose a brand that is canned in juice, not syrup. Even light syrup will unnecessarily add large amounts of sugars and calories to this high-protein, low-calorie drink.

1 cup blanched, sliced almonds
1 cup lite vanilla soy milk
4 large fresh peaches, diced, or 1 can peaches (15 oz., in juice), drained
1 Tbs. honey (if using fresh peaches)
2 Tbs. low-fat plain yogurt
4 ice cubes

Place all the ingredients in a blender and process until smooth. Serve cold.

Kilocalories:	231	Protein (g):	8	Carbohydrate (g):	23
Fat, total (g):	14	Cholesterol (mg):	1	Saturated Fat (g):	1.2
Monounsaturated Fat (g):	8.6	Polyunsaturated Fat (g):	3.4	Dietary Fiber, total (g):	4
Sugar, total (g):	18	Sodium (mg):	47	Potassium	333
Vitamin A (RE):	42	Vitamin C (mg):	4	Calcium (mg):	82
Iron (mg):	1	Vitamin D (μg):	0	Vitamin E (mg):	8
Thiamin (mg):	<0.5	Riboflavin (mg):	<0.5	Niacin (mg):	2
Pyridoxine (mg):	<0.5	Folate, total (μg):	12	Cobalamin (μg):	<0.5
Biotin (μg):	<0.5	Pantothenic Acid (mg):	<0.5	Vitamin K (μg):	<0.5
Phosphorus (mg):	154	Magnesium (mg):	80	Zinc (mg):	1
Copper (mg):	<0.5	Manganese (mg):	1	Selenium (μg):	2
Protein (%):	12	Carbohydrate (%):	37	Fat (%):	51

Spinach and Avocado Salad
with Warm Shiitake Balsamic Vinaigrette

SERVES 4

This recipe is a mix of cool green salad and a warm dressing. This combination eases the tartness of the spinach and gives it a delightfully mild taste. The balsamic vinegar's flavor is tamed and enhanced by the flavors of shiitake and sunflower seeds. This salad makes a tasty and healthy meal or a great side dish for an Italian dinner.

**1 avocado, diced
1 Tbs. lemon juice
8 cups baby spinach
2 Tbs. olive oil
4 cloves garlic, minced
2 Tbs. hulled sunflower seeds
⅓ cup fresh, finely chopped shiitake mushrooms
3 Tbs. balsamic vinegar
Pinch of sea salt**

1. Coat the diced avocado with lemon juice to prevent discoloration.
2. Arrange the avocado and spinach beautifully in a large plate or a salad bowl.
3. Heat the olive oil in a small saucepan over medium-high heat. Add the garlic and sunflower seeds, and cook for 1 minute or until golden. Add the shiitake mushrooms and cook for 1 minute or until tender.
4. Carefully add the balsamic vinegar and sea salt, and as soon as the mixture starts to boil, remove from the heat, immediately pour the dressing over the spinach salad, and serve.

Kilocalories:	173	Protein (g):	4	Carbohydrate (g):	9
Fat, total (g):	15	Cholesterol (mg):	0	Saturated Fat (g):	2.0
Monounsaturated Fat (g):	8.9	Polyunsaturated Fat (g):	2.7	Dietary Fiber, total (g):	5
Sugar, total (g):	2	Sodium (mg):	92	Potassium	671
Vitamin A (RE):	429	Vitamin C (mg):	23	Calcium (mg):	74
Iron (mg):	2	Vitamin D (µg):	0	Vitamin E (mg):	4
Thiamin (mg):	<0.5	Riboflavin (mg):	<0.5	Niacin (mg):	2
Pyridoxine (mg):	<0.5	Folate, total (µg):	155	Cobalamin (µg):	0
Biotin (µg):	4	Pantothenic Acid (mg):	1	Vitamin K (µg):	259
Phosphorus (mg):	101	Magnesium (mg):	72	Zinc (mg):	47
Copper (mg):	9	Manganese (mg):	1	Selenium (µg):	4
Protein (%):	8	Carbohydrate (%):	20	Fat (%):	72

Broccoli and Brussels Sprouts with Balinese Peanut Sauce

SERVES 8

This vitamin-E-enhanced version of the popular Indonesian appetizer gado-gado is sure to be a hit at any gathering. Gado-gado is a mix of quickly boiled vegetables, including cabbage, bean sprouts, carrots, and long beans, dressed with a spicy peanut sauce. For a dinner party, try serving this tropical-inspired dish in a large banana leaf, folded over and tied on top with a string of banana leaf fiber.

Pinch of sea salt
15 brussels sprouts, trimmed of stems and wilted leaves
Florets of 2 heads broccoli (approx. 20 oz.)
½ cup crunchy peanut butter, preferably low sodium
1 Tbs. low-sodium soy sauce
1 tsp. red chili paste (sambal) or ½ tsp. ground cayenne pepper

½ Tbs. brown sugar
Juice of 1 lime
¼ cup hot water plus 1 Tbs. additional, as needed
¼ cup chopped peanuts

1. Blanch the brussels sprouts in salted boiling water for 4 minutes. While the brussels sprouts are still cooking, set a steamer on the top of the pot and cook the broccoli for 4 minutes or until both brussels sprouts and broccoli are tender. Be careful not to overcook the vegetables. Set aside the broccoli. Drain the brussels sprouts well and cut in half lengthwise.
2. Place the peanut butter, soy sauce, chili paste (or cayenne), brown sugar, lime juice, and hot water in a large mixing bowl and whisk vigorously or until smoothly blended.
3. Add the broccoli and brussels sprouts and coat with sauce evenly to season. Serve on a plate, top with chopped peanuts.

Kilocalories:	158	Protein (g):	9	Carbohydrate (g):	11
Fat, total (g):	11	Cholesterol (mg):	0	Saturated Fat (g):	2.0
Monounsaturated Fat (g):	5.0	Polyunsaturated Fat (g):	3.1	Dietary Fiber, total (g):	5
Sugar, total (g):	4	Sodium (mg):	51	Potassium	507
Vitamin A (RE):	144	Vitamin C (mg):	95	Calcium (mg):	60
Iron (mg):	2	Vitamin D (μg):	0	Vitamin E (mg):	4
Thiamin (mg):	<0.5	Riboflavin (mg):	<0.5	Niacin (mg):	3
Pyridoxine (mg):	<0.5	Folate, total (μg):	94	Cobalamin (μg):	0
Biotin (μg):	<0.5	Pantothenic Acid (mg):	1	Vitamin K (μg):	207
Phosphorus (mg):	147	Magnesium (mg):	59	Zinc (mg):	1
Copper (mg):	<0.5	Manganese (mg):	<0.5	Selenium (μg):	3
Protein (%):	19	Carbohydrate (%):	26	Fat (%):	55

Pinto Bean and Kale Soup

SERVES 4

This hearty but low-cal soup can be served hot or cold. The clear soup, chunky vegetables, and beans are so filling that you may just want to skip the bread. For the busy body, make a potful on a weekend, refrigerate, and reheat for a healthy dinner in a hurry.

1 Tbs. olive oil
2 cloves garlic
1 cup chopped white onion
1 can (16 oz.) pinto beans, drained and carefully rinsed under running water
1 can (14 oz.) low-sodium chicken broth
2 cups water
1 dried bay leaf
2 medium tomatoes, diced
Pinch of sea salt
Freshly ground black pepper
¼ tsp. chili powder
5 cups chopped kale, stems and center ribs removed

1. Heat the olive oil in a large pot over medium-high heat. Add the garlic and cook for 1 minute or until it starts to sizzle. Add the onion and cook for 3 minutes, stirring, or until tender and slightly golden.
2. Add the pinto beans and stir to coat with oil. Add next seven ingredients, from chicken stock to chili powder. Bring to a boil. Reduce the heat to low and cook, covered, for 10 minutes or until the tomatoes are tender and the flavors are blended.

3. Increase the heat to high, stir in the kale, and cook, covered, stirring occasionally, for 5 minutes or until the kale is tender.

Kilocalories:	205	Protein (g):	10	Carbohydrate (g):	33
Fat, total (g):	5	Cholesterol (mg):	0	Saturated Fat (g):	0.8
Monounsaturated Fat (g):	2.8	Polyunsaturated Fat (g):	1.0	Dietary Fiber, total (g):	8
Sugar, total (g):	7	Sodium (mg):	445	Potassium	860
Vitamin A (RE):	796	Vitamin C (mg):	117	Calcium (mg):	184
Iron (mg):	4	Vitamin D (μg):	0	Vitamin E (mg):	2
Thiamin (mg):	<0.5	Riboflavin (mg):	<0.5	Niacin (mg):	2
Pyridoxine (mg):	<0.5	Folate, total (μg):	109	Cobalamin (μg):	0
Biotin (μg):	3	Pantothenic Acid (mg):	<0.5	Vitamin K (μg):	690
Phosphorus (mg):	182	Magnesium (mg):	72	Zinc (mg):	1
Copper (mg):	<0.5	Manganese (mg):	1	Selenium (μg):	10
Protein (%):	19	Carbohydrate (%):	60	Fat (%):	21

Healthiest Meat Loaf

SERVES 8

A much healthier version of the classic meat loaf, this recipe uses lean beef combined with wheat germ. The beautiful green swirls produced by the spinach on the cut surface of this dish make it attractive for dinner parties. Forget Mom's recipe; impress your family and guests with this lower-calorie meat loaf that is a breeze to make!

Olive oil spray
5 cups spinach, tightly packed
1 cup wheat germ
½ lb. 5–7% fat ground beef
½ cup cooked brown rice
1 egg or ¼ cup cholesterol-free egg substitute

1 cup finely chopped onion
½ cup finely chopped bell pepper
2 cloves garlic, minced
2 Tbs. fresh parsley
¼ tsp. dried thyme
¼ tsp. ground nutmeg
½ tsp. canola oil
3 Tbs. tomato sauce, divided
6 Tbs. Worcestershire sauce, divided
⅓ cup ketchup

1. Preheat the oven to 350°F.
2. In an olive-oil-coated skillet, cook the spinach over high heat for 3 minutes, or until most of the liquid is evaporated. Set aside.
3. Place all the remaining ingredients except 1 Tbs. of the tomato sauce, 3 Tbs. of the Worcestershire sauce, and the ketchup in a large bowl. Mix well until evenly combined.
4. On a working surface, place a 12-by-15-inch piece of plastic wrap. Spread the beef mixture to a rectangular shape measuring ⅛-inch thick, 10 inches wide and 14 inches long. Spread the spinach evenly over the beef mixture.
5. Starting with the 10-inch side, carefully roll up jelly-roll fashion, making one pinwheel-shaped roll.
6. Transfer to an olive-oil-coated baking dish and bake for 40 minutes.
7. In the meantime, combine 1 Tbs. of the tomato sauce and 1 Tbs. of the Worcestershire sauce. Brush over the meat loaf and bake for 20 more minutes.
8. Combine the remaining 2 Tbs. Worcestershire sauce and the ketchup. Serve on the side.

Kilocalories:	151	Protein (g):	12	Carbohydrate (g):	17
Fat, total (g):	4	Cholesterol (mg):	44	Saturated Fat (g):	0.9
Monounsaturated Fat (g):	1.3	Polyunsaturated Fat (g):	1.1	Dietary Fiber, total (g):	3
Sugar, total (g):	5	Sodium (mg):	234	Potassium	487
Vitamin A (RE):	165	Vitamin C (mg):	19	Calcium (mg):	50
Iron (mg):	3	Vitamin D (μg):	<0.5	Vitamin E (mg):	4
Thiamin (mg):	<0.5	Riboflavin (mg):	<0.5	Niacin (mg):	3
Pyridoxine (mg):	<0.5	Folate, total (μg):	100	Cobalamin (μg):	1
Biotin (μg):	3	Pantothenic Acid (mg):	1	Vitamin K (μg):	83
Phosphorus (mg):	248	Magnesium (mg):	74	Zinc (mg):	4
Copper (mg):	<0.5	Manganese (mg):	<0.5	Selenium (μg):	12
Protein (%):	32	Carbohydrate (%):	45	Fat (%):	23

Spice-Rubbed Grilled Chicken with Hazelnut and Grape Sauce

Serves 4

You will be pleasantly surprised at how nicely this unique combination of sweet grapes and choice spices accentuated by aromatic hazelnut blends in your mouth. This colorful dish—bright red spice, light green grapes, and brown sauce poured over the chicken breasts—looks almost as good as it tastes.

2 Tbs. ground sweet paprika
1 tsp. dried thyme
1 tsp. chili powder
Pinch of sea salt
4 4-oz. chicken breasts
Olive oil spray
1 Tbs. olive oil
2 cups seedless green grapes, halved
3 Tbs. white grape juice

2 Tbs. dry white wine
⅓ cup low-sodium, fat-free chicken broth
½ cup blanched hazelnuts, chopped (if blanched are not available, heat in the oven at 350°F for 10 minutes or until brown skins begin to flake; place on a dish towel, fold it over the nuts, and rub vigorously to remove the skin)

1. Combine the paprika, thyme, chili powder, and sea salt in a large bowl.
2. Coat the chicken breasts with olive oil spray and place in the spice bowl, coating evenly. Place in the refrigerator until ready to cook.
3. In a medium saucepan, heat the olive oil over medium-high heat and add the grapes. Cook for 3 minutes or until steam starts to rise.
4. Add the grape juice, white wine, and chicken stock and bring to a boil. Reduce the heat to medium and cook for 18 minutes. Transfer to a blender and process on low pulse, just until grapes are broken evenly.
5. While the sauce is cooking, coat a nonstick skillet with olive oil spray and heat over medium-high heat. Add the chicken and cook for 2 minutes, or until one side is cooked and golden; turn and cook for another 2 minutes. Reduce the heat to medium and cook for an additional 3 minutes on each side, or until thoroughly cooked.
6. Pour the sauce over the chicken—about ⅓ cup for each—and top with 2 Tbs. of hazelnuts.

Kilocalories:	352	Protein (g):	30	Carbohydrate (g):	21
Fat, total (g):	16	Cholesterol (mg):	66	Saturated Fat (g):	1.6
Monounsaturated Fat (g):	10.6	Polyunsaturated Fat (g):	2.4	Dietary Fiber, total (g):	4
Sugar, total (g):	17	Sodium (mg):	124	Potassium	658

Vitamin A (RE):	167	Vitamin C (mg):	14	Calcium (mg):	61
Iron (mg):	2	Vitamin D (μg):	0	Vitamin E (mg):	5
Thiamin (mg):	<0.5	Riboflavin (mg):	<0.5	Niacin (mg):	13
Pyridoxine (mg):	1	Folate, total (μg):	21	Cobalamin (μg):	<0.5
Biotin (μg):	2	Pantothenic Acid (mg):	1	Vitamin K (μg):	7
Phosphorus (mg):	290	Magnesium (mg):	65	Zinc (mg):	1
Copper (mg):	<0.5	Manganese (mg):	2	Selenium (μg):	21
Protein (%):	34	Carbohydrate (%):	24	Fat (%):	41
Alcohol (%):	1				

Almond and Sunflower Seed Crusted Tuna with Spinach Sauce

SERVES 4

The powdered almonds and sunflower seeds form a tasty and crunchy crust for this tuna dish. Make sure to pan-sear the tuna lightly and to leave the center slightly undercooked to prevent it from becoming too dry. The freshest tuna may be found in your local fish market and can be identified by its bright red color and firm edge.

1 lb. sushi-grade fresh tuna steak, 1 inch thick (could be in a couple of separate steaks)
Pinch of sea salt
Freshly ground black pepper
¼ cup sliced almonds
½ cup hulled sunflower seeds
2 Tbs. finely chopped fresh parsley
½ tsp. coriander seeds
½ tsp. cumin seeds
½ tsp. ground cayenne pepper
1 egg white

½ Tbs. olive oil
1 cup tightly packed spinach
1 Tbs. low-sodium soy sauce
1 Tbs. rice vinegar
1 tsp. extra-virgin olive oil

1. Sprinkle the tuna with sea salt and black pepper evenly.
   Place in a container and refrigerate.
2. Process the next six ingredients (from almonds to cayenne
   pepper) in a blender until all the nuts and spices are
   combined and powdered. Transfer to a large mixing bowl.
3. Whisk the egg white lightly in a large mixing bowl. Dip
   the tuna in the egg white, then coat with the nut mixture.
4. Heat the ½ Tbs. olive oil in a skillet over medium heat.
   Add the tuna and cook for 4 to 5 minutes on each side.
   This leaves the tuna slightly undercooked with a bright
   red center.
5. In the meantime, process the spinach, soy sauce, rice
   vinegar, and extra-virgin olive oil in a blender until
   smooth.
6. Transfer the fish to a cutting board and slice carefully with
   serrated or Japanese knife into ½-inch slices. Arrange the
   slices symmetrically on a large plate and drizzle with the
   spinach sauce.

Kilocalories:	342	Protein (g):	33	Carbohydrate (g):	7
Fat, total (g):	21	Cholesterol (mg):	43	Saturated Fat (g):	3.0
Monounsaturated Fat (g):	8.1	Polyunsaturated Fat (g):	8.2	Dietary Fiber, total (g):	3
Sugar, total (g):	1	Sodium (mg):	258	Potassium	588
Vitamin A (RE):	838	Vitamin C (mg):	6	Calcium (mg):	61
Iron (mg):	3	Vitamin D (µg):	0	Vitamin E (mg):	12
Thiamin (mg):	<0.5	Riboflavin (mg):	<0.5	Niacin (mg):	12

Pyridoxine (mg):	1	Folate, total (µg):	69	Cobalamin (µg):	11
Biotin (µg):	3	Pantothenic Acid (mg):	2	Vitamin K (µg):	57
Phosphorus (mg):	527	Magnesium (mg):	114	Zinc (mg):	2
Copper (mg):	1	Manganese (mg):	1	Selenium (µg):	56
Protein (%):	38	Carbohydrate (%):	8	Fat (%):	54

Oriental Mustard Green and Tofu Stir-Fry

SERVES 4

This easy-to-make dish is both delicious and nutritious. The phytoestrogen and vitamin-packed soybean tofu is combined with mustard greens, which contain more vitamin E than most other fresh vegetables. Shichimi (literally "seven-spice powder") is a traditional Japanese spice made of chili, sansho or Japanese pepper, black and white sesame seeds, perilla or Japanese basil, laver, and hemp seeds. This unique spice has been used in Japanese recipes for centuries; it can be found in most Asian or Japanese grocers' spice sections under the brands House or S&B.

Canola oil spray
2 eggs or ½ cup cholesterol-free egg substitute, beaten
1 Tbs. canola oil
1 clove garlic, minced
1 Tbs. minced ginger
10 oz. water-packed firm tofu, torn into 10 cubes (use your hands)
4 cups chopped mustard greens
1 Tbs. sake Japanese rice wine
1 Tbs. low-sodium soy sauce
¼ tsp. shichimi seven-spice powder

1. Heat a nonstick skillet over high heat and coat with canola spray. Cook the eggs for 30 seconds to 1 minute. Transfer to a plate and set aside.
2. Wipe the skillet clean and heat the canola oil. Over high heat, add the garlic and ginger and cook for 1 minute or until slightly golden.
3. Add the tofu and cook for 4 minutes or until golden, turning occasionally.
4. Stir in the mustard greens and cook for 2 minutes or until tender.
5. Add the sake and soy sauce, then cook for 2 minutes, stirring, or until the liquid is absorbed by the tofu. Turn off the heat and stir in the cooked egg and shichimi powder. Serve warm.

Kilocalories:	118	Protein (g):	11	Carbohydrate (g):	4
Fat, total (g):	5	Cholesterol (mg):	<0.5	Saturated Fat (g):	0.5
Monounsaturated Fat (g):	2.4	Polyunsaturated Fat (g):	2.4	Dietary Fiber, total (g):	2
Sugar, total (g):	<0.5	Sodium (mg):	221	Potassium	317
Vitamin A (RE):	370	Vitamin C (mg):	40	Calcium (mg):	327
Iron (mg):	2	Vitamin D (μg):	0	Vitamin E (mg):	7
Thiamin (mg):	<0.5	Riboflavin (mg):	<0.5	Niacin (mg):	1
Pyridoxine (mg):	<0.5	Folate, total (μg):	110	Cobalamin (μg):	2
Biotin (μg):	—	Pantothenic Acid (mg):	1	Vitamin K (μg):	100
Phosphorus (mg):	319	Magnesium (mg):	70	Zinc (mg):	1
Copper (mg):	<0.5	Manganese (mg):	<0.5	Selenium (μg):	9
Protein (%):	40	Carbohydrate (%):	13	Fat (%):	43
Alcohol (%):	4				

Tropical Granola

MAKES 8 CUPS, SERVES 16

Skip the chocolate bar and jump right into this healthy sugar-craving buster. A true orchestra of antioxidant-rich foods, all it entails is tossing the ingredients together, putting the mixture on a cookie sheet, and baking. When placed in an airtight container, this tropical granola can remain fresh for up to a month. For a late-night snack, wash it down with vanilla-flavored soy milk.

4 cups old-fashioned rolled oats
1 cup wheat germ, raw
½ cup sliced almonds
¼ cup flaxseeds
1 cup hulled sunflower seeds
⅓ cup canola oil
⅓ cup honey
⅓ cup water
1 tsp. ground cinnamon
1 cup chopped dried mango

1. Preheat the oven to 350°F.
2. Combine the rolled oats, wheat germ, almonds, flaxseeds, and sunflower seeds in a large mixing bowl. Divide the mixture in half and spread evenly over two baking pans. Bake for 12 to 15 minutes or until slightly brown.
3. Combine the canola oil, honey, water, and cinnamon in a small mixing bowl. Remove the pan from the oven and pour the canola mixture over the oat mixture, then mix—along with the dried mango—until thoroughly and evenly coated.

4. Reduce the oven heat to 300°F and bake for an additional
   30 minutes, stirring every 10 minutes to cook evenly.
   Remove from the oven and cool to room temperature.
   Store in an airtight container at room temperature for up
   to 4 weeks.

Kilocalories:	268	Protein (g):	8	Carbohydrate (g):	32
Fat, total (g):	14	Cholesterol (mg):	0	Saturated Fat (g):	1.2
Monounsaturated Fat (g):	5.4	Polyunsaturated Fat (g):	6.0	Dietary Fiber, total (g):	6
Sugar, total (g):	12	Sodium (mg):	3	Potassium	293
Vitamin A (RE):	39	Vitamin C (mg):	2	Calcium (mg):	40
Iron (mg):	2	Vitamin D (µg):	0	Vitamin E (mg):	8
Thiamin (mg):	<0.5	Riboflavin (mg):	<0.5	Niacin (mg):	1.4
Pyridoxine (mg):	<0.5	Folate, total (µg):	62	Cobalamin (µg):	<0.5
Biotin (µg):	1	Pantothenic Acid (mg):	1	Vitamin K (µg):	7
Phosphorus (mg):	298	Magnesium (mg):	85	Zinc (mg):	2
Copper (mg):	>0.5	Manganese (mg):	1	Selenium (µg):	14
Protein (%):	12	Carbohydrate (%):	45	Fat (%):	43

Blueberry and Peach Crisp

SERVES 8

This great summer treat consists of fresh berries and peaches coated with wheat germ and sugar. Try it with low-cal frozen yogurt ice cream, soy ice cream, or regular yogurt topped with finely chopped mint leaves.

3 large peaches
Canola oil spray
3 cups blueberries
3½ Tbs. whole wheat flour
¾ cup wheat germ

¼ cup turbinado sugar
1½ Tbs. canola oil
¼ tsp. vanilla extract

1. Preheat the oven to 350°F.
2. Chop the peaches into ½-inch, bite-sized cubes. Place in a canola-sprayed, 8x8-inch baking dish along with the blueberries.
3. Sprinkle 2 Tbs. of the whole wheat flour over the fruits and mix to coat.
4. In a small mixing bowl, combine the remaining ingredients and cover the fruits.
5. Bake for 20 minutes or until the topping is golden brown and the liquid of the fruits bubbles. Remove from the oven and let stand for 10 minutes before serving.

Kilocalories:	134	Protein (g):	4	Carbohydrate (g):	24
Fat, total (g):	4	Cholesterol (mg):	0	Saturated Fat (g):	0.2
Monounsaturated Fat (g):	1.7	Polyunsaturated Fat (g):	1.5	Dietary Fiber, total (g):	4
Sugar, total (g):	13	Sodium (mg):	6	Potassium	257
Vitamin A (RE):	26	Vitamin C (mg):	10	Calcium (mg):	15
Iron (mg):	1	Vitamin D (μg):	0	Vitamin E (mg):	4
Thiamin (mg):	<0.5	Riboflavin (mg):	<0.5	Niacin (mg):	1
Pyridoxine (mg):	<0.5	Folate, total (μg):	44	Cobalamin (μg):	<0.5
Biotin (μg):	1	Pantothenic Acid (mg):	<0.5	Vitamin K (μg):	5
Phosphorus (mg):	132	Magnesium (mg):	42	Zinc (mg):	2
Copper (mg):	<0.5	Manganese (mg):	<0.5	Selenium (μg):	3
Protein (%):	11	Carbohydrate (%):	65	Fat (%):	24

Appendix B

Resources

Alzheimer's Association
National Headquarters
919 North Michigan Avenue, #1000
Chicago, IL 60622-1676
(800) 272-3900
http://www.alz.org

A national voluntary health organization that funds Alzheimer's disease research, advocates for changes in public policy, and provides comprehensive public information on services, programs, and publications as well as contact information for local chapters in major U.S. cities.

Alzheimer's Disease Education and Referral Center (ADEAR)
P.O. Box 8250
Silver Springs, MD 20907-8250
(800) 438-4380
http://www.alzheimers.org/adear

A clearinghouse of information on Alzheimer's disease, including drugs in clinical trial, abstracts of educational materials, and research reports funded by the National Institute on Aging.

Alzheimer's Disease Europe
145 Route de Thionville
L-2611 Luxembourg
http://www.alzheimer-europe.org

An organization of European Alzheimer organizations; its Web site provides information on Alzheimer's disease and rare forms of memory problems, and offers tips for caregivers.

Alzheimer's Disease International
45–46 Lower Marsh
London SE1 7RG
United Kingdom
44-20-7620-3011
http://www.alz.co.uk

The umbrella organization of the Alzheimer's associations of more than sixty member countries; its Web site provides information on the causes, diagnosis, and treatment of Alzheimer's disease and links to Web sites of Alzheimer's associations around the world.

American Geriatrics Society (AGS)
The Empire State Building
350 Fifth Avenue, Suite 801
New York, NY 10118
(212) 308-1414
http://www.americangeriatrics.org

A professional association of physicians and other health professionals who specialize in the health care of older adults; its Web site provides public policy news and health links of interest to older people.

Administration on Aging (AOA)
330 Independence Avenue SW
Washington, DC 20201
(202) 619-7501
http://www.aoa.gov

An agency of the U.S. Department of Health and Human Services that provides home- and community-based support for older people, including preventive health, nutrition, and transportation services; its Web site provides information on services, support, and assistance available for seniors, including those afflicted with Alzheimer's disease.

American Association of Retired Persons (AARP)
601 East Street NW
Washington, DC 20049
(800) 424-3410
http://www.aarp.org

A nonprofit organization of individuals over age fifty; its Web site provides information of interest to older Americans, including senior legislation and health policy news and a health and wellness newsletter.

Clinical Trials
http:/www.clinicaltrials.gov

A service of the National Institutes of Health (NIH) and the Food and Drug Administration (FDA) that provides up-to-date information on federally and privately funded clinical trials for a wide range of diseases and conditions.

CenterWatch Clinical Trials Listing Service
22 Thomson Place, 36T1
Boston, MA 02210-1212
(617) 856-5900
http://www.centerwatch.com

A publishing and information services company that provides information on clinical research trials sponsored by the pharmaceutical and medical device industries.

National Center for Complementary and Alternative Medicine (NCCAM)
NCCAM Clearing House
P.O. Box 7923
Gaithersburg, MD 20898
(888) 644-6226
http://nccam.nih.gov

A branch of the National Institutes of Health (NIH) that supports research on complementary and alternative healing practices; its Web site provides reliable information on many CAM treatments organized by therapy and by disease conditions. It also provides important consumer alerts and public health advisories on potentially harmful dietary supplements and herbal medications.

National Institute on Aging (NIA)
Building 31, Room 5C27
31 Center Drive, MSC 2292
Bethesda, MD 20892
(301) 496-1752
http://www.nia.nih.gov

A branch of the National Institutes of Health (NIH) that supports research on the aging process and age-related diseases; the Web site provides information on the latest scientific research on aging and a directory of organizations of interest to older people.

National Institute of Mental Health (NIMH)
NIMH Public Inquiries
6001 Executive Boulevard, Room 8184, MSC 9663
Bethesda, MD 20892-9663
(301) 443-4513
http://www.nimh.nih.gov

A branch of the National Institutes of Health (NIH) that conducts and supports research on the brain, behavior, and mental disorders; the Web site provides breaking research news and clinical trials on Alzheimer's disease, depression, schizophrenia, and other diseases.

National Institute of Neurological Disorders and Stroke
P.O. Box 5801
Bethesda, MD 20824
(800) 352-9424
http://www.ninds.nih.gov

A branch of the National Institutes of Health (NIH) that conducts and supports research on neurological diseases, including Alzheimer's disease, Parkinson's disease, and stroke; its Web site provides an information page in frequently asked questions (FAQ) format for an extensive list of brain and nerve diseases.

Index

About the Author

Zaldy S. Tan, MD, MPH, is a respected clinician, researcher, and educator. He received his training from Brown University and Harvard Medical School. As the director of The Memory Clinic at Beth Israel Deaconess Medical Center, Harvard Medical School, and a research investigator at the Framingham Heart Study, he has diagnosed thousands of patients with degenerative brain conditions. He is an expert in the recognition of the earliest signs of memory problems and finding the most effective interventions based on sound scientific evidence.

Dr. Tan's research focuses on the risk and preventive factors for Alzheimer's disease and ways to achieve successful aging. He is on the faculty of medicine of Harvard University and a research scientist at the Massachusetts Institute of Technology's Agelab. His research has received national and international coverage. He has presented the results of his research at major national conferences. He also regularly gives talks on Alzheimer's disease and memory improvement techniques.

Dr. Tan lives in Cambridge, Massachusetts.